Redefining Perfect

Redefining Perfect

The Interplay Between Theology & Disability

Amy E. Jacober

FOREWORD BY
Nick Palermo

 CASCADE *Books* • Eugene, Oregon

Cascade Books
An Imprint of Wipf and Stock Publishers
199 W. 8th Ave., Suite 3
Eugene, OR 97401

www.wipfandstock.com

PAPERBACK ISBN: 978-1-4982-3310-1
HARDCOVER ISBN: 978-1-4982-3312-5
EBOOK ISBN: 978-1-4982-3311-8

Cataloguing-in-Publication data:

Names: Jacober, Amy E. | Foreword by Palermo, Nick

Title: Redefining perfect : the interplay between theology and disability / Amy E. Jacober.

Description: Eugene, OR: Cascade Books, 2017 | Includes bibliographical references with index.

Identifiers: ISBN 978-1-4982-3310-1 (paperback) | ISBN 978-1-4982-3312-5 (hardcover) | ISBN 978-1-4982-3311-8 (ebook)

Subjects: LCSH: People with disabilities—Religious aspects—Christianity. | Theological anthropology. | Title.

Classification: BT732.7 .J35 2017 (print) | BT732.7 (ebook)

Manufactured in the USA   12/04/17

For all of my friends needing to be reminded that God has *always* included them. Thank you for teaching me over the years.

CONTENTS

FOREWORD

I N 1986, YOUNG LIFE began a ministry to youth with disabilities known as Capernaum. We didn't have a guidebook; we simply knew these youth were created in God's image and they needed to know Jesus, too.

Thirty years later, accessibility to public spaces—education, buildings, even the digital world—is typical. The church and theological community however, are still lagging behind. Sixteen years into the twenty-first century and the church is in need of a theology regarding persons with disabilities and a corresponding hospitality. It is time for the church to wrestle with the inclusion of all people, typical or not, and to wrestle with theology and the reality of disability.

In 2004, Young Life's Capernaum pioneered a week of camp, bringing together 100 kids with disabilities, 100 able-bodied kids, and a group of leaders. Our leadership team needed extra help, and one of the persons who stepped forward was Dr. Amy Jacober.

Amy and I became fast and deep-spirited friends. I watched her serve at this camp with a profound sense of wonder. I discovered what I would only come to know in a deeper way over the next twelve years. She is a woman with a superb mind and a tender, generous heart. She is a woman who knows how to dance with theology and praxis, and she has been teaching me that very dance in our twelve-year friendship.

As a pastor and passionate lover of Jesus and people, Amy ministers with and to kids with disabilities. She has been a trusted conversation partner as we sought ways to continue growing in our ministry to and with persons with disabilities. As a skilled theologian, Dr. Jacober has done the deep study of Scripture and history and brought together the praxis and critical analysis needed to form a cohesive theology with a disability lens.

Some years ago, I came across a painting in a market in Germany, a painting of persons in wheelchairs dancing with typical dance partners. The swirls of colors and the interplay of the persons and the dance captivated me. (I would share the painting with you but the work is unsigned.) This book provides a narrative to that image. It is a manual of the dance between disability and theology. What I would have given for a book like this when I began my ministry!

This book leads us to consider the nature of life for those with disabilities as it relates to faith. It reveals to us our failure to consider disability within the Scripture which leads us down the road of a "disabled theology." This book is where a deep knowledge of the Scriptures meet a deep knowledge of those with disabilities. That result is a holy dance that leaves us all more complete in understanding how God intended it for individuals and faith communities.

As you read, I pray in God's providence that he places someone with a disability in your life, that will allow you to read this book in a very personal manner. I pray that if you have a disability, that you are encouraged and experience a deep sense of inclusion. If you are a minister or caretaker already involved, may this encourage and serve as a tool to open conversation for further inclusion. Read on. You are about to be challenged and engaged!

Nick Palermo

Founder, Young Life Capernaum Ministry
Co-Executive Director, Emmaus Inn Ministries
Author, *Missing Stars, Fallen Sparrows*

ACKNOWLEDGMENTS

S OMEONE RECENTLY ASKED HOW long I have been writing this book. The honest answer is that it has been in the making for more than fifteen years. It may not be that I had put down any words or concepts, but it has been there, forming and reforming with a thousand conversations, camps, ministries, and moments where I witnessed my friends with disabilities being included and sadly, at times, excluded. I lost count of how many times I pitched the idea for a book on theology and disability only to be told there was no market for it. Several years have passed and times are changing. I am grateful in many ways for the delay in publication for what I offer today is far more mature than my enthusiastic but embryonic thoughts of years ago. Still, there is room to grow. It is my hope that this will be just the beginning of conversations for some. It is my prayer that others who read this will take the ideas further to honor God and remind us all that those who are too often marginalized are the most Christ-focused of us all.

The intensity of my past couple of years would seem exaggerated were I to offer an account here. Suffice it to say, this book would never have made it if not for my tribe who served as supporters, cheerleaders, helpers, readers, chefs, and babysitters. For each, I am profoundly grateful. The first among many would be my very own littles, Sedona, Keliah, and Deaglan, who teach me more about the art of hospitality and inclusion than anyone else I know. I'd also like to thank my father, John Jacober, who stepped in to help create space for me to write on more days than I could count; my mom, Betty Jacober, whose unending love sustains me; my mother-in-law Carolyn Peacock, who rearranged weeks of her time to be with the kids so I could write. Joyce del Rosario provided much needed sustenance for marathon jags of writing in the form of prayers, encouraging texts, and a delivery of meals so I didn't have to divide my attention on precious days of writing.

ACKNOWLEDGMENTS

Mindi Godfrey offered unending wisdom and practical advice. Nick Palermo was the first to say out loud, years ago, that I needed to write this. He never gave up cheerleading me on even on days when I was unsure. David Thames, whose grace in allowing our entire family to serve in the Phoenix NE Young Life Capernaum club, is astounding. Megan Grey-Hering always seems to know how to send fairy dust for a little magic when I need more hours than a day could hold. Tio Jesse Villegas, who took the kids for all day adventures to allow me time to work. Carolyn and Richard Vash, who taught me that a quadriplegic is far from helpless or pitiful and grew into lifelong family by choice. For each of you, I am grateful.

Finally, I could not have done this without my husband, Cory Peacock. There are no words that could come close to expressing how grateful I am for you in my life. You, above all others, have been my partner, editor, child wrangler, and biblical advisor. As iron sharpens iron, I am better for having had your support. You helped me to articulate more clearly what I struggled to put in words. Thank you.

Rev. Amy Jacober, PhD, MDiv, MSW

1

INTRODUCTION

Are you in or are you out?

> "Remember that God is writing a story in your lives as you minister in his kingdom, but your story takes on meaning because it is part of an eternal story."—Paul Hiebert

IDEAS OF PERFECT SEEM to be everywhere. Every night I look at my own children as I tuck them in and we say prayers. I am filled with wonder that I get just a little time with them and as they drift to sleep, I think they are perfect. I daydream of what they will be like in the years ahead and fear the day they ask for a tattoo, or worse, just show up with one. This is not because I dislike tattoos but because at their tender age their skin is beautiful, so perfect. Note that I did not say flawless. I know every bump and scar they each have. In waking hours, I hear angst pouring from my seven-year-old when she can't master a task immediately and bursts into tears saying, "It's not perfect!" I hear the rips of paper as my five-year-old shows me a drawing that looks to my eyes like every other drawing she has done but she declares, "It is not perfect." I, then, come to comfort my three-year-old as he sobs, rolled in a ball next to a pile of Lego blocks that he can't transform into the picture he holds in his mind and he says, "It's terrible, it's not perfect."

I could list my own litany of struggles with perfection: my insecurities for looks and talent growing up; my insecurities for being smart enough to know I was not the smartest person in the room during my PhD program; and my struggles to fit in and be "perfect" when I was the only female faculty in my department and the youngest faculty member by far. I would be nearly paralyzed by my anxiety to produce academic articles that were worthy of anyone else's time and not merely padding my CV. Many articles, as a result, were left unfinished. I sought perfection in everything I could control, knowing so much was out of my control. Yet, this often left me missing out on the messy fun that is life.

The church should have been the place to garner a little perspective, but it only brought more anxiety over the concept of perfection. As a young child I was told how much God loved me and enjoyed being with me. Then, just as hormones and adolescent cliques were kicking in, I was told that I fell short, that I didn't have what it took to be God's beloved anymore, and that I needed to repent of all that I had done to separate myself from the one who, I was told, would always love me. Turns out, I was not the only one to hear this paradoxical message, the three-pronged message that says (1) you are exactly who you need to be, yet (2) you still fall short, and (3) it is up to you to repent and fix "it," even if you don't know what "it" is.

Perfect can be even more complicated for my friends with disabilities. The message from the world seems to point out every way in which they don't measure up or aren't viewed with the same value as typical people. This message comes in a thousand small ways, from the space between racks in a store being too narrow for wheelchairs or crutches, to the un-wanted stares and taunts for their appearance, or noise, or leg braces. Many of my friends don't see others like themselves in the movies or shows they watch, the books they read, or the places they visit. They see the same pol-ished, airbrushed, flawless people we all see.

For my friends with disabilities, the church, too, should and could be a place to hear a different perspective. Unfortunately, we have a long history of language and practice that was never intended to exclude, but exclude it does. As we have become more aware of disability in recent years, the conversations have begun in some circles for what this means for the church. Still other conversations that I have experienced firsthand are too often laced with comments that say things like, "this is what we believe . . . unless you have a disability." Such comments carry the subtext of special dispensation for persons with disabilities. As gently as I have been able, I explain that a foundational truth of the church doesn't work that way. We do not get to say here is what is truth, unless it doesn't apply to you. When many well-meaning people look at doctrines, the concern is their purity, their perfection, rather than in what ways God's people were impacted. Un-less the doctrine can include those with disabilities, their family, friends, and communities as they are, then the work is not finished. The onus is on us in the church to remain true to Scripture, the work of the church, and the guiding of the Holy Spirit to name and then live doctrinal truths that open doors for everyone regardless of ability.

Long before airbrushing for magazine covers and the barrage of media focusing on the external, we had the church and those seeking to follow God longing for perfection. This notion sounds good. It's what we have learned and internalized. The difficulty comes in our understanding of the word *perfect*. It comes reconciling our understanding of *perfect* with the message of *perfect* in Scripture. It comes in the ways in which *perfect* has been interpreted culturally over the centuries. There are several words in the Bible for the term we translate as *perfect* in English. In our English-speaking, Western mind-set, *perfect* carries with it the connotations of flawless, the ideal, lacking nothing, and a sense of extremes. The most frequently used word in the Old Testament that is translated perfect is *tamim* (Ps 101:2, Job 1:1). It can be understood to be without blemish or spot, with moral integrity. The cognates carry with them the notion of "spiritual wholeness and uprightness, especially as one is in right relationship to God, [which] reflect a relational/ethical perfection that is patterned after the character of God."[1] In the New Testament we find *telos* (Col 1:28), which carries with it the idea of design, end, or purpose. We also find *teleios* (Jas 1:3–4, Matt 5:48), which brings the ideas of complete or lacking nothing. Another word used is *katartizo* (Eph 4:13, Heb 31:21), meaning moral integrity, a communal aspect of wholeness and completeness that comes from spiritual unity. And one more word is *holokleros* (1 Thess 5:23, Jas 1:4) talking of someone who is spiritually sound and needing nothing for completeness. Perfection has a clear presence across the arc of scripture. It however is not about being flawless or ideal, it is about being complete, whole, and having spiritual integrity. It is about having the right attitude in pursuit of God and living the life taught and modeled by God.

Over the centuries, the interpretation of these Scriptures and the concept of perfection have taken a varied and winding path. At times, it became about knowing (cognitive assent) all a person could humanly know about God. There was a time when perfection was viewed as withdrawing from the world and devoting oneself to prayer. Taken to an extreme, in some circles perfection became about retreating from reality and entering into a euphoric space with God alone. For some, perfection was thought to be attainable here on earth, while for others it was attainable only in the eschaton. As time progressed, again in *some* circles, the notion of perfection

---

1. Elwell, ed., *Evangelical Dictionary of Theology*, 902.

was reserved only for clergy or those who had devoted themselves to a monastic life. Following this separation of clergy and lay people, the pendulum swung back so that all people had access to perfection. This, too, has taken on a variety of forms but what was lost along the way was the notion that perfection is about an interaction and relationship with God more than external appearance or presence.

Perfection in the church today has an uneasy place in our theology. Most of us know better than to say out loud that anyone is expected to be perfect, as in flawless. Instead, what we communicate is presented in the accessibility of our buildings, the illustrations we use in teaching, the examples of those who are serving, and the very presence of those who are placed in leadership and service positions. These pragmatic actions have behind them a history of theology that has been inconsistent in embracing and empowering those with disabilities. In fact, some of our theology has done more harm than good for those with disabilities. They have been seen as less than human, were chosen to endure tremendous physical and emotional pain to glorify God, and were viewed as a project or object lesson for those who were able-bodied—to name just a few injustices people with disabilities have suffered at the hands of the church. The more I studied and taught theology, the more I realized there was an entire people group being shut out. I began the process of thinking through doctrines in light of each doctrine's meaning in and for the lives of those with disabilities and their family and friends. What I discovered in seeking an inclusive yet still sound theology was not a theological perspective exclusively for people with disabilities alone. It simply was a better theology for all of us. What applied to someone with a disability also applied to the typical person. It neither required exceptions nor hindered typical people. By thoughtfully considering those with disabilities, this new statement of theology simply included more people than it had previously. Too often, doctrinal statements could be compared to a building without a ramp at the entrance. It cannot accommodate a wheelchair or someone unable to do steps. Yet, a building with a ramp is open to all, whether typically or differently abled. No walking person ever refused to enter a building because it had a ramp. Nor were they denied access to the building for not having a chair of their own. In this book I present several doctrines viewed through the hermeneutical lens of disability. This is the ramp to the building called theology.

Theology and Disability

It is a daunting task even to try to write theology. It is so much better lived than written. Yet the written word allows conversations across distances in space and time. The written word invites slow moments of reflection and pondering. Living theology is breathed in and out like the air around us. This book will attempt to capture that which fills our lungs with life and hope, preserving it for longer than the moment it occurred, inviting conversation from those who have not had the same interactions, and creating space for the deepest hospitality to shape who we are with one another and with God.

There is no single accepted definition of disability. We cannot begin to attempt to address all of the variations of disabilities, whether manifested at birth or acquired in life, that include the physical, intellectual, mental, and emotional domains. John Swinton offers a fantastic guiding definition of disability: "Disability is not defined by any particular impairment or difference. What forms the core of 'disability' is the recognition of a shared experience of oppression, marginalization, and injustice."[2] This definition is particularly jarring for those of us in the church. It speaks to our understanding about God and who we are to be as the people of God. While attitudes about disability are changing, we all have a long way to go. This writing is but one step along that path, inviting people to be more particular about their choice of words when it comes to expressing and living theology.

This book is a conversation about the intersection of theology and disability. It is not a theological treatise, an exhaustive work of systematic theology, or exclusively a practical how-to ministerial book. It is a look at several major theological components that have excluded, isolated, or ghettoized those with disabilities over the centuries. We are all a product of the culture and time in which we live and for many of the great theologians on whose shoulders we stand, the concept of disability was just not in their worldview. If only it had been! I imagine many great atrocities could have been avoided. In our time, however, there is a decades-long conversation regarding disability that is taking place in our schools, public spaces, governments, and hospitals. Except for a handful of extraordinary churches, the conversation of disability is just now entering the church. This book can serve as a primer to the disability conversation and invitation to you to continue and expand the conversation.

2. Swinton, "Disability, Ableism, and Disablism," 445.

When I first started thinking about how to include those with disabilities in ministry, I assumed I was writing little exceptions to theological doctrines that would result in the inclusion of people with disabilities. What I soon discovered is that I was just writing and living better theology. I do not mean to suggest it was better than other theologians. Rather, it was better than the earlier version of my own traditional theology. It better represented and included the breadth and depth of the members of God's kingdom. When we intentionally include people with disabilities, it is amazing how others outside of the traditional places of power are included, too: women, people of color, different ages, and cultures. I am certain this theology can still improve, but for today, it is more inclusive and representative of what God wants for and from us.

I never intended to write a book on theology and disability. The need to write this book bubbled up after years of conversations. I was constantly advocating for the inclusion of teenagers with disabilities and their families in youth ministry. I didn't have a grand reason why I sought inclusion. I just resonated with the underdogs. The more I advocated, the more conversations I ended up in. The more conversations I had, the more I began noticing when those with disabilities were not, or *too often* were not, being included. Initially, I suggested a course on theology and disability at the seminary where I was teaching. I was told there was no need for something so specialized. I suggested workshop after workshop at the major youth ministry trainings across the country on the topic of ministering to those with disabilities, only to be told there was no interest. I pitched articles and books on disability to every major Christian publishing house for over a decade, only to be told there was no market. No need. No interest. Feeling rejected and frustrated, I just started to weave the conversation into every course I taught: theology, pastoral care, crisis, leadership . . . you name it. While I didn't love how it happened, the result was brilliant. The topic of disability was not relegated to a special interest course for those few already inclined to take the course. Disability was a fact of life and important in every aspect of ministry. Through conversations with friends, adolescents, parents, colleagues, and yes, many students, the questions I seek to address in this book arose. Questions like, "Can people with disabilities really sin?" Or, "Did God make a mistake with some people?" Or, "Is it OK to baptize someone with a disability?" The questions weren't the practical ones I anticipated. I had thought I would address issues like how to provide accommodations, or learning about medicines and allergies. The questions were theological. They got to the core of what we, as Christians, believe and it messed with people's faith. These questions over the years have taken on a life of their own. This is my attempt to tell the story of that life.

Revelation

Years ago I was attending a panel session on theology and disability at the American Academy of Religion. There were several leaders up front in dialogue with one another. The idea was that we in the audience were getting to witness a great conversation regarding theology and disability and what that might mean for the church. At the end of the session, the moderator opened up the conversation to anyone in the room to ask questions for the panel's insights. There were many good questions, a lot of conversation, and a lot of terms being discussed as if they really mattered. The most significant moment I recall came from an exchange between a mother of a special needs child and Stanley Hauerwas. The mother told the story of her child being raised in a church where it was common upon confirmation to be baptized or have an infant baptism reaffirmed. Her daughter went through the classes and wanted to be baptized just like her friends. The church leadership held a meeting, convened a committee, and tasked the pastor with informing the mother of their decision. The pastor said they would be happy to pray for her daughter, but she was not a candidate for baptism because they believed she did not understand the meaning of baptism. This act was so sacred, they rationalized, that baptism itself would be defiled should it be administered to anyone who had less than a full understanding of what was taking place. Baptizing a person with a disability, they argued, would cheapen the sacred duty of the church to administer such a ritual. Through tears she told of her daughter's love for Jesus and of her daughter's insatiable desire to be at church and serve others. Her daughter was understanding of the church's position and wanted to stay at that church, but the mother, just could not stay. She still believed in God, but didn't have the theology to figure out what was taking place with her daughter. She hoped that somehow that individual church was screwed up, but she had not, as of that time, found a place that would love her daughter the way she believed God did. When she finished her story, she asked the panel what she should do. In a way that only Hauerwas can, he responded in what was simultaneously the most and least pastoral manner possible. He said something close to the following. "She should be baptized because who the hell really knows what is happening in that moment!"[3] Hauerwas went on to say that perhaps, just perhaps, that a child with a disability understands better than anyone of us what is taking place. As he or she may be unencumbered with the details of getting the words just right and instead, such a child could be fully present with God in that moment. Hauerwas also went on to say that the church had better do the hard work theologically to address the full inclusion of all who are created in the image of God.

This hard work is the task at hand. It must begin with a look at how we know what we know. At this point in history, we have hundreds of years and thousands of pages of reflection on God, the church, and doctrinal stances. Each work is an oral and written outpouring given with a desire to live more faithfully. Each work realistically is a product of its own time. Karl Barth very famously rejected the notion that theology was to adapt to culture. He was pushing against a system where the church supported World War II. He pushed even more strongly when he denounced church leaders who would not speak against the Nazis so that they might get along well with the governmental leaders. His was a world where he was not always afforded the luxury of nuance. As such, Barth took a strong stand. Barth's position on the intersection of theology and culture remains influential. The cracks in many theological statements, however, are beginning to show when we consider their lack of inclusion for persons with disability. When we see that society at large is more inclusive towards our friends with disabilities than the church is, theologians must address the gaping holes and poorly worded writings of the past that relegate those with disabilities to a position of marginalization, oppression, isolation, and abuse. Let me be clear, I am not adapting theology to the worldwide trend of better treatment for and inclusion of those with disabilities. I am simply advocating that we catch up with what has always been biblically and theologically present, seeking a better theology that also addresses the wide spectrum of disability.

Seeking a better theology requires knowing how we will know what we know. The two most common ways of knowing within Christianity are through general revelation and special revelation. General revelation is the older of the two, existing long before the written word. It allows for

3. An interesting statement that could seem glib or ill-informed were it from someone other than a seasoned, revered theologian. Stanley Hauerwas is the emeritus Gilbert T. Rowe Professor of Theological Ethics at Duke Divinity School and was named "America's Best Theologian" by *Time* in 2001. He is one of the best-regarded theologians alive today. While he writes on a wide variety of topics, he is well known for addressing issues of theology and disability.

the movement of the Holy Spirit's faithfulness beyond what can be known directly from Scripture. It is also highly suspect to many faithful believers and theologians who are concerned that it can be held captive by cultural shifts, leading away from Christianity and toward ever-increasing distortions of God's truth. Special revelation is what God revealed in and through Scripture. Scripture gives us in written words the most full picture of who God is and how God wants us to live. It is also a product of God's inspiration, written at specific times, in specific places, addressing specific circumstances. It was an oral tradition long before it was a canonical collection of texts. It was lived and passed down in ways where all had access to the revelation and all had the ability to access it to the best of their abilities in the life choices they made. This book embraces both kinds of revelation. Both general and special revelation allow us to be a more faithful people seeking a God-honoring relationship with the creator of the universe and one another, no exceptions.

And yet, for centuries, exceptions *have* been made. Those with disabilities have not been fully included or considered in the writings and ministries of the church. Revelation, both general and special, was reserved for the elite of the Christian community and society. Throughout this writing, some of the theological positions that exclude those with disabilities will be named and addressed. This struggle is nothing new.[4] What is new to the church at large is an attitude of receptiveness and a long overdue, widespread desire to include both by what *is* said and done and by what *is not* said and done.[5] There have been numerous comments and exceptions throughout the years of theological writing regarding those with disabilities within the broader context of theology. But a theology that is *by design* inclusive of those with disabilities is emerging.

While not apparently his intention, Emil Brunner offered a look at revelation that is helpful for the inclusion of those with disabilities. Brunner argued that revelation centered on absolute mystery and *could not* be acquired

---

4. For brief history of disability studies and typology as well as a detailed look at an iconic biblical story concerning disability see Schipper, *Disability Studies and the Hebrew Bible*.

5. I am using the term *inclusion* here intentionally moving beyond welcome. This will be unpacked in the section on hospitality, but for now suffice it to say that welcome is a first step that affords a greeting. Inclusion however, makes room at the table and values the voice, both in substance and delivery, of those with disabilities. It allows light to be shed in dark places as the reality of God is revealed in and through the lives of those with disabilities.

as one acquires ordinary knowledge.[6] He believed the task of revelation was to move us from being lost in the dark to light in a way that could only be God revealing Godself. Thus, humanity is transformed not by acquiring knowledge about God but by God's transformative act. In fact, "Brunner makes it clear that revelation is not primarily about increasing knowledge but about the transformation of persons and the destructive forces of evil."[7] This matters! It is not how much one knows about God. It is whether one knows God! For every time the question is asked, "Does someone with a disability 'get it'?" I can only imagine a resounding groan and eye roll from God, frustrated that we in ministry and the church too often just don't get that it's not about what you know, but who you know. The "what" of God— the details and facts and adiaphora—is important, conversation-worthy, and secondary. It is not the core of revelation. So the question of whether one "gets it" is the wrong question. The question must stem from a better pneumatology where we let go of our anxiousness and allow the Holy Spirit to reveal Godself to all people in ways that build relationships, liberate from darkness, and transform the destructive forces of evil.

God's revelation is neither a set of beliefs nor doctrines requiring intellectual assent. Nor is it a blind leap of faith. The revelation of God paradoxically reveals God and affirms the very hiddenness of God. Daniel Migliore says this beautifully. "In God's self-revelation God has become identifiable, yet God is never fully comprehensible."[8] Echoes of Hauerwas's statement to the mother asking about her child ring out in this declaration. The more we know God, the more we realize there is more to know. We simply do not know all there is to know and never will this side of glory. That does not invalidate our knowledge. "Confession that God has been revealed, however, is altogether different from the claim to know every-thing about God or to have God under our control. When God is revealed, God remains God and does not become a possession at our disposal."[9] I fully agree with Migliore when he writes, "The claim to total knowledge is emphatically rejected by postmodern philosophers and theologians, who believe all such claims are inherently arrogant and inevitably lead to op-pression of one sort or another."[10] For those statements and practices that

6. For more on this see Brunner, *Revelation and Reason*.

7. Erskine, "How Do We Know What To Believe?," 46.

8. Migliore, *Faith Seeking Understanding*, 24.

9. Ibid.

10. Ibid., 23–24.

have required intellectual assent to validate the work of God in the lives of an individual and community, oppression and unintended exclusion have often been the result. A corrective is needed. For some people with disabilities, intellectual assent as we currently understand it will not be possible. That does not mean they do not know God. In fact, it may be that God reveals himself in ways that are more clear to those with disabilities. Here, I humbly present a work that is both intellectual and rigorous while simultaneously acknowledging that it is not the final word on God's revelation. We need one another to best piece together the fragments of human knowing that includes knowing God.

As God is revealed, we get to come together and benefit from the inclusion of all. The inclusion of those with disabilities ought not be charity work nor self-serving hedonism. It is simply what God intended all along and we are just now catching onto. Thomas Reynolds proposes what he calls a "dramatic metaphorical reversal" when he "inverts the scheme of the cult of normalcy by privileging disability."[11] He goes on to write of disability as being baseline, not inferior or broken. Reynolds also notes that we have been created to be interdependent on one another in different seasons of our lives and for differing lengths of time. He is careful to state that in no way is he disparaging those who have real-life, daily struggles whether physically, cognitively, or emotionally. Rather he upends the traditional paradigm, making disabilities the norming norm from which to approach all life, including faith and interaction. He states:

> We are inherently relational creatures who need each other to become ourselves. That is we are unfinished and deficient unto ourselves. And this highlights our insecurity and weakness, undoing the illusion of security gained from being inscribed with body capital within the cult of normalcy. Seen in this light, disability is no fringe issue. Through it emerges a more holistic picture of what it means to be a person. When privileged and brought from the margins to the center, disability deconstructs the cult of normalcy and opens the possibility of wider human solidarity.[12]

The cult of normalcy has often kept those with disabilities on the margins of society. Deborah Creamer also calls into question the cult of normalcy with a critique of an understanding of limits that emerge from disability. Creamer draws a distinction between limits and limitations.

11. Reynolds, *Vulnerable Communion*, 104.
12. Ibid., 105.

Limits are a part of the human condition. For example, I am short and often ask others around me to reach something from a high shelf. It is part of my human condition to interact and rely on others or some other accommodation, like a chair or step stool, in order to reach items far above my head. My shortness is a limit, not a limitation. The particular challenges that accompany disabilities, likewise, should be viewed as limits. Creamer writes, "our limits need not (and ought not) be seen as negative . . . they are an important part of being human."[13] Creamer and Reynolds not only call for the cult of normalcy to be upended but join a chorus of others who have been naming this for years in practice. Nick Palermo, founder of Young Life's Capernaum ministry, has said repeatedly that "we all have disabilities, it's just that some show more than others."[14] Palermo has also declared that each of us has gifts and graces to offer to the community. We may all contribute in big and small ways with each having the capacity to serve in a way that suits particularities providing a reciprocal relationship of serving. This interaction of service makes it possible to encounter God.[15] Alasdair MacIntyre refines this concept from the vantage point of an academician, writing:

> We need others to help us avoid encountering and falling victim to disabling conditions, but when, often inescapably, we do fall victim, either temporarily or permanently, to such conditions as those of blindness, deafness, crippling injury, debilitating disease, or psychological disorder, we need others to sustain us, to help us in obtaining needed, often scarce, resources, to help us discover what new ways forward there may be, and to stand in our place from time to time, doing on our behalf what we cannot do for ourselves. Different individuals, disabled in different ways and degrees, can have their own peculiar talents and possibilities, and their own difficulties. Each therefore needs others to take note of her or his particular condition. And this is one of the points at which it is important to remember that there is a scale of disability on which we all find ourselves. Disability is a matter of more or less, both in respect of degree of disability and in respect of the time periods in which we are disabled. And at different periods of

13. Creamer, *Disability and Christian Theology*, 64.

14. Capernaum is a division of Young Life with a focus on teens with disabilities. It was founded by Nick Palermo in 1986.

15. Nick Palermo is a personal friend and mentor. While not specifically published, he has been sharing these concepts with all who would listen as he has served in ministry for decades as a practitioner leader.

our lives we find ourselves, often unpredictably, at very different points on that scale. When we pass from one such point to another we need others to recognize that we remain the same individuals that we were before making this or that transition.[16]

MacIntyre declares that we are all disabled, but the scale is different for each person. On that scale of disability, another scale is created, one which describes the degree and time in which we need one another to live into our own peculiar talents and possibilities while having to live realistically with our own peculiar difficulties. It is with this in mind that we embrace the truth of interdependence. Sara Ellet says it this way: "I see God as merciful enough to allow this world to have constant reminders of our collective need for each other."[17] We simply cannot exist without one another and each of us is equally important as the other, no exceptions.

It is this kind of interdependence that allows God's revelation to come to the center of our Christian interaction. Perhaps most famously this was lived by Henri Nouwen among his friends at L'Arche Daybreak with Adam Arnett and Bill Van Buren. As an esteemed and accomplished professor, writer, and priest, Nouwen chose instead to slow down and learn to live what he had been professing to believe. While Nouwen was unquestionably a gift to his community, it is in this community that he learned to listen to others and God. It was through the friendships Nouwen lived with those with disabilities that he was taught and guided on how to come out of his own dark night of the soul and encounter God through revelation once again. At his low point, Nouwen had all of the information one could ever hope to have, but missed God. It was through interactions with his friends with disabilities that he was once again able to see what God had been try- ing to reveal all along.[18] Ellet echoes this sentiment and expands on it. She says, "Hearing from the Holy Spirit is often a mystery as well as hearing the desires and needs of other humanity. I have come to understand that to hear the Holy Spirit or a Core Member, one must listen with their entire self. I have to listen to their body, to what they are not saying, and to the words. I have to listen to their history and their desire for a future. The same is true of the Holy Spirit. It must be heard in all possible ways to be in

16. MacIntyre, *Dependent Rational Animals*, 72–73.

17. Sara Ellet, Director of Professional Service for L'Arche Clinton, personal com- munication, September 29, 2016.

18. See henrinouwen.org for more information from the Henri Nouwen Society on his life with those with disabilities and writings over several decades of ministry.

community with God."[19] All Christians must learn to listen to our friends who may communicate differently lest we miss profound messages from God.

Not only must we listen, but we must also communicate. The seminary I attended still felt the influence of a legendary professor generations after his death. T. B. Maston was an ethicist who trained at Yale and was clearly capable of writing at the most sophisticated levels, yet had two mitigating factors in his life. The first was his mother, who was not thought to have had but a third-grade education. "By his own account, Maston typically evaluated the articles, Sunday School lessons, and even books he wrote by this simple criterion: 'Is this written so that my mother could read and understand it?'"[20] The second influence was his son, Tom, who was born in 1925 with complications that resulted in crippling cerebral palsy. Maston and his son had a deep and abiding reciprocal relationship. Maston lived not so that others may be impressed with the sacrifices made for his son, but because it was the right thing to do. Maston wrote not so that those around him would be impressed with how smart he was, but so they might better understand the revelation of God.

What follows is my attempt to imitate Maston's example so others may see and know God in ways that include everyone, in particular those with disabilities. I did not create this work from nothing. It has been in the making through my own faith journey and education long before I knew it was to be written. It has been influenced and built from numerous classes, professors, thousands of pages of reading, hours of prayer, and days of doing life with friends with disabilities. I stand on the shoulders of great Christians who were thinkers and writers who came before me. Any credit for this writing is deserved by many named and unnamed in these pages; any mistakes are mine alone. In the following pages will be not an exhaustive systematic theology, rather a re-envisioning of several doctrines with the intentional inclusion of those with disabilities. In what has turned out to be one of the greatest surprises since I began thinking and writing in this area more than ten years ago, I have gained friends and a deeper relationship with God. May this also be true for those who read this book.

19. Sara Ellet, Director of Professional Service for L'Arche Clinton, personal communication, September 29, 2016.

20. Maston, *Both-And*, 251–52.

Questions for Reflection and Ministerial Application

1. What are your presuppositions about disability?

2. In what ways has this introduction challenged your presuppositions?

2

GOD

Who do you say I am?

> "The problem of practicing the Christian life, however, is that God is not always obvious."—Michael Battle

> "The Christian God is not a lonely God, but rather a communion of three persons."—Miroslav Volf

EVEN THOSE OF US who love God may find ourselves in circumstances that try us to the point of feeling either abandoned by God or like we clearly got who God is wrong. I am not talking about a walking away from faith. Rather, I am referring to those Job-like seasons of life where it seems like no matter how faithful we are, all the areas of our lives begin to fall apart and we can't but help wonder, in our most honest moments, if God really can do anything, wants to do anything, or even cares. We tend to think good Christians aren't supposed to say those things out loud. If and when we do, we are chastised for those questions instead of invited into a conversation to discover or rediscover just who God is.

For many people and families impacted by disability, conversations with God frequently include the word *why*. Why me? Why my child? Why this disability? Why does the world handle disabilities this way? God can handle the questioning. Later in this book we will address the connection between struggle and hope. Here, though, there needs to be a baseline understanding of just who God is. Understanding who God is does not remove the daily struggles of living with a disability, but a false understanding of God burdens our hearts and stresses our souls. A false understanding of God leads families to question what horrible thing they did to deserve this, and leads a person with a disability to wonder if God loves them or even finds them to be worthy of love. A false understanding of God elevates the utility of individuals, honoring the typically abled to the detriment of those with disabilities. A false understanding of God can lead to negative public sentiment, prohibitive public action, and punitive public policy that denies the value of all whom God has created.

A clear example of faith shaping public life comes from Dietrich Bonhoeffer's 1933 visit to a village named Bethel. Bonhoeffer was going in order to gain insight on a collective writing project that would name the true marks of the church. This village contained an institution that cared for the most fragile and mentally ill of society. The motivation for the care given in the institution was distinctly Christian. That this service took place in Nazi Germany is remarkable. Still more remarkable was the village's willingness to care for, protect, and speak out against a society that was using its power and ideology as justification for isolating, experimenting upon, and killing those with disabilities. This is the backdrop that informed the following quote from Bonhoeffer's *Ethics*:

> Life created and preserved by God possesses an inherent right, completely independent of its social utility . . . . There is no worthless life before God, because God holds life itself to be valuable. Because God is the Creator, Preserver, and Redeemer of life, even the poorest life before God becomes a valuable life.[1]

While this quote is full of theological ideas deserving attention, it is specifically Bonhoeffer's declaration of who God is that concerns us here. Because of who God is, God alone has the authority to declare that which is valuable or not, and God declares all lives, including those with disabilities, to be valuable.[2] With this as a presupposition, we must understand who this God is, this God who finds value in every life.

Trinity

God within a Christian context is a Trinitarian God, three in one. The *Shema*, found in Deuteronomy 6:4, grounds Jews and Christians today in

1. Wannenwetsch, "My Strength is Made Perfect in Weakness," 353.

2. While God declares all to be of value, the reality is that there is a social construction of disability where the dominant society neither ideologically nor pragmatically embraces this declaration of value. As Christians, we should be different. For further discussion on this topic and practical steps forward, see Tumeinski and McNair, "Social Role Valorization." This is discussed further in chapter 6.

monotheistic belief. God is One, no more, no less. Christians, though, have to ask, "But what about Jesus and the Holy Spirit?" In antiquity, the idea of the Trinity was debated to determine how the Trinity was to be understood. The doctrine of Trinity was set in place at the Council of Nicaea in 325 CE. Even then, the doctrine's establishment was accomplished with a great deal of struggle and controversy. It is still difficult to comprehend and discuss this concept today. It is a paradox that can defy logic and demand faith. To add to the degree of difficulty, the term *Trinity* is never mentioned in scripture. The concept, however, is undeniable. Millard Erickson offers a series of questions that highlight the need for establishing a Trinitarian theology. These include: Whom are we to worship? To whom are we to pray? Is the work of each in isolation or in collaboration? Who participated in the work of God on the cross and subsequently the resurrection? Is there a hierarchy in the Trinity?[3] I would add the question: What does it mean to be created in the image of God in light of the Trinity? We are not aiming here for a comprehensive understanding of the Trinity. I hold to a traditional Christian view of the Trinity and the essential elements of this doctrine as we turn to the godhead and the distinctive work associated with each member. These essential elements include the unity of God; the deity of each of the three persons; that each is of the same substance, not similar substance to each other; that the Trinity is eternal; and finally that there is a mutual indwelling known as the perichoretic relationship that allows for distinct activity with the participation of each member without subordination or hierarchy being established.

The account of creation itself affirms the doctrine of the Trinity and the goodness of those with disabilities. Genesis 1:26–27 states, "Then God said, 'let us make humankind in our image, according to our likeness . . . . So God created humankind in His image, in the image of God He created them; male and female He created them."[4]

This could be written with helpful notes as follows: "Then God [singular] said, 'let us [plural] make humankind [plural] in our [plural] image, according to our [plural] likeness." God is both singular, supporting our monotheistic claims, and plural, supporting our Trinitarian claims. Each member of the Trinity is intimated in the traditional Scriptures explaining

3. Erickson, *Christian Theology*, 322.

4. The omitted section of Scripture discusses that over which humanity was to have dominion. This is discussed in the chapter on theological anthropology as I look at the distinction between dominion and mastery. In this chapter, the point is to consider the implications within our understanding of the Trinity.

the origins of creation. In other words, from the beginning, the Trinity is present and at work. It follows then that it is the Trinity who declares what is so often attributed to God the Father, that creation is good. God is the creator and in the creation account we see repeatedly the declaration by God that what has been created is good. Each member of the Trinity offers a consistent declaration, all of humanity is created, all of humanity is created in the likeness of God, and all of humanity is good. There are no mistakes, no mishaps, no exceptions.

Understanding who God is and knowing God are two separate things. It is possible, in fact probable, to begin an authentic relationship with God before fully understanding who God is. As with all relationships, it is in the actuality of the relationship that deeper understanding takes place. I know my husband, but it has taken a decade for me to understand certain things, and even years into the relationship I learn something new almost every day. How much more so with God? Within the Christian tradition there are certain attributes that have come to be accepted regarding God. These attributes, which are God's very nature, are permanent and inseparable from God's essence. Even still, God's self-revelation is not exhaustive and leaves us with the ability to both know God and confidently declare how great and incomprehensible is God.

Many people find the task of considering the attributes of God to be tedious or even unnecessary. But without careful consideration, God's attributes can be forgotten or twisted. For those with a disability or those of us who care deeply for those with disabilities, this has had detrimental effects over the years. Disabilities have been categorized as everything from abhorrent and unacceptable to a blessing and a God-glorifying, special gift. Both extremes ignore who God is and the reality of those living with disabilities. It is in understanding who God is that we can better understand how to live Christianly in relation to those with disabilities. God cannot help but be consistent with all creation. There is no person more loved, more valuable, more precious than the next. Each person is loved and a just life is desired for them by God. It is in the following attributes we find a partial yet powerful understanding of God: immanence, transcendence, purity, holiness, righteousness, justice, integrity, genuineness, truthfulness, faithfulness, love, benevolence, grace, mercy, and persistence.[5] For those

5. This particular list was taken from *Christian Theology* by Millard Erickson. The concepts however may be found in any number of theology books or in volumes dedicated to each attribute itself. Each attribute has particular implications and could comprise a work on its own regarding the implications for those with disabilities. For this book, an

concerned with issues facing those with disabilities and the impact of disabilities on our churches, families, communities, and society, this list of attributes becomes our plumb line. When tempted to take the easy path or offer the easy explanation about what God wants for our lives, a healthy understanding of the attributes of God ensures that our arguments remain true to God's character.

A deeper discussion of the unique persons in the Godhead requires a choice of language. For this book, we will use Father, Son, and Holy Spirit. This choice is made following the explicit proximity of these terms in Matthew 28:19. Language, pronouns in particular, are problematic and God cannot be confined within the limitations of our words. Having already established a grounding in the Trinity, that males and females have been made in the image of God, I will proceed with writing assuming that God is inclusive of gender as we currently understand it. For now, as with the actual mechanics and details of the Trinity, it remains a mystery that is largely incomprehensible.

Father

In Scripture, names often served more than just the function of being able to call someone by a distinct label. Names carried weight and meaning. They identified something about the person or the parents, something wished for the person, something that described an action or attribute. When it comes to God, the first encounter we have recorded with this concept of name is Moses at the burning bush where we learn the name of God is "I AM." This is both less than helpful and profound at the same time. It is difficult to wrap our minds around. In talking with a friend recently, I asked her how having a brother with Down Syndrome had impacted her view of God. Her response echoes that of Exodus 3:14. She wrote to me, "I think knowing Tim shows me so clearly how God does BIG BEAUTIFUL things with the most unlikely characters. I think it shows me how small our minds are in terms of trying to understand His bigger plans and reasons for His diverse creation."[6] Increasingly this ambiguous response of God being "I AM" is a reminder that God is more than any of us have ever imagined.

More frequently used, though, than the mysterious name of "I AM," God is portrayed as Father. We see this throughout Scripture. In

acknowledgement of their import will suffice.

6. Liz Tatlow, personal communication, September 23, 2016.

Deuteronomy 32:6b, "Is not he your father, who created you, who made you and established you?" In Malachi 2:10, "Have we not all one father? Has not one God created us? Why then are we faithless to one another, profaning the covenant of our ancestors?" In Matthew 6:26, "Look at the birds of the air; they neither sow nor reap, nor gather into barns, and yet your heavenly Father feeds them. Are you not of more value than they?" These are just a few of the many occurrences. God as a parent figure is a powerful metaphor. It is an intimate term. It is a term that connotes creation, care, and long-suffering on our behalf. God is the father who looks down and sees, not as anyone else in the world sees their child, but with the holy love of a parent seeing the beauty of each child and all of his or her potential. God sees far beyond any ability or disability, to the core of our very being, and names it as precious. For every person with a disability, God is both big and powerful, while simultaneously intimate and personal. God is immanent and transcendent.

Son

Most of us are able to relate to Jesus more than other members of the Trinity. We are taught in childhood that Jesus, in many respects, was just like us. We are taught that Jesus ate, drank, got sleepy, had friends, liked to play, and had relationships with his family. We read of Jesus getting angry at the temple and needing to get away from crowds after a long day of work. For many, Jesus is the guy to whom we can all relate. We say out loud, of course, that he was perfect and we are not . . . but what is most often communicated is that he was just a typical person. It is the motif of the *typical* person that leaves out the relatability factor for many people with disabilities.

It is in the broken body of Jesus that inclusion is modeled. It is in Jesus that God incarnate is disabled. It is on the cross where Jesus struggles to breathe, his lungs collapsing under the weight of his own body, hanging publicly in shame. It was on the cross where Jesus is fully present in what would have been considered not only unclean in that he died, but even in the very way he died. Paul, in Galatians 3:13, understands the curse levied is not just around the taboo of a dead body but that his body was accursed for experiencing the capital punishment reserved for the worst of society, as laid out in Deuteronomy 21:22–23. McClendon offers a great deal of insight:

Christ, being crucified, actually became such an unclean, untouchable one, since he died on a cross meant for barbarian criminals. Therefore he broke the barrier of such insider-outsider exclusion, redeeming those who loved him from all 'curse' laws. It is not that God cursed Christ and had him crucified. Rather, it is that Christ, by taking his place as one accursed (hanged or crucified) broke through that 'curse' rule; Disciples certainly could not count Christ 'accursed.' Having taken his beloved body down from the cross, how were they to reckon him, or anyone else in that same humbling fix, unclean or 'accursed'?[7]

For all who have felt accursed, who have been labeled as less-than or unacceptable, what Jesus does on the cross is break the curse. With the curse broken, those who have been treated as accursed in this life may experience a victory over the sin inflicted upon them. It is at the resurrection that Jesus presents himself with wounds on his hands, feet, and side. These are wounds that would have rendered him lame and altered his grip. These wounds were not just for show, they were available to be touched in a time and place when this very act would have rendered the typical person touching these wounds unclean. It is a potent role reversal of what is read in Matthew 8:3. In this passage Jesus first touches the leper, and only after touching him, which violates ancient Israelite codes of cleanliness, Jesus declares the leper to be clean. Nancy Eiesland views God not as "an omnipotent self-sufficient God, but neither a pitiable, suffering servant. In this moment, I beheld God as a survivor, unpitying and forthright. I recognized the incarnate Christ in the image of those judged 'not feasible,' 'unemployable,' with 'questionable quality of life.'"[8] In this one act of appearing and being touched, Jesus is declaring those with differently abled bodies acceptable and clean in every sense of the term. He even went so far as to enter into their reality, naming people with disabilities as viable, valuable, and able to participate in a high quality of life.

Jesus was frequently in the habit of declaring an upside-down kingdom. Since he is a member of the Trinity, such an act comes with the weight and authority of the one who created it. It seems unlikely that Jesus would upturn his own vision of the kingdom. It seems more likely that humanity flipped what God had intended, and it was Jesus who arrived to set the proper understanding of kingdom back in order. The question may arise, is this even possible? Does Jesus have the same authority to declare as clean

7. McClendon, *Doctrine*, 218.
8. Eiesland, *The Disabled God*, 89.

that which God the Father has declared clean. The answer is a resounding yes. This yes was affirmed in 325 at the Council of Nicaea where Jesus was declared to be *homoousios* (of the same substance) with the father as opposed to *homoiousios* (of a similar substance) with the father. Jesus is God. Therefore he has the same authority to declare anything or anyone clean.

Importantly, Jesus is both God and is disabled. It is an acquired disability, as many are, but it is a disability nonetheless. For all the times when Jesus is preached as perfect, we would do well to revisit the beginning of this book where perfect was set in its biblical context. Perfect is not about being flawless or without blemish. It is about being whole and spiritually sound. Jesus as the disabled God elevates the status of all those with disabilities to a place of deep identification. Jesus offers a model not of one who is to be pitied or hidden, but one who is powerful in weakness and unencumbered by the expectations of this world.

Holy Spirit

Perhaps the most difficult person of the Trinity to discuss, the Holy Spirit is vibrant and mysterious. Phyllis Tickle poses the question and answer regarding the Holy Spirit as follows: "How does the Holy Spirit work in any era? . . . In every time and place, the Spirit—that is God—is about movement/disruption and change/transformation."[9] Tickle goes on to discuss how it is the experience of the Holy Spirit, not the learned doctrines and catechetical teachings, that speak new life in unexpected places. I cannot but help to think of a woman I met several times a few years ago. She has a severe form of autism and in her own words is left disastrously without friends. She is smart. She is able to understand all that goes on around her, but her body simply does not cooperate, making communication nearly impossible. She tells of a teacher who helped her learn how to use her speaker board with her physically uncooperative body, allowing her to communicate for the first time. After the initial release of frustration regarding years of being hidden in plain sight, she tells of her communion with God. She tells of lengthy conversations with the Holy Spirit and relates a level of understanding most faithful believers will never experience. The pain of being isolated from the world was real. So, too, was the depth of her relationship with God. As technology progresses, we are finding more and more that those with disabilities are not to be the pitied recipients of

9. Tickle, *The Age of the Spirit*, 117.

charity. Rather, they are necessary if we all are to hear from the Holy Spirit for the disruption and transformation God has for his people.

The mystery of the Holy Spirit comes in the very qualities that define her. The Holy Spirit is unable to be predicted and yet fully deity; worthy of praise and worship, yet often overlooked; present from all eternity and named in the councils as the third member of the godhead, yet in many ways only recently being accepted as a necessary member of the Trinity. The Holy Spirit offers both comfort and conviction as appropriate. Amos Yong writes, "the Holy Spirit creatively enables and empowers our full humanity in relationship to ourselves, others, and God, even in the most ambiguous situations."[10] The brilliance of Yong's statement is the declaration of the work of the Holy Spirit to bring about full humanity for all people, those who are able to interact with others, with themselves, and importantly with God. Not all people are able to know themselves as they are known. In fact, for some, this would be detrimental. In a world that mocks differences, or panders to an infantilizing of adults with cognitive disabilities, Yong explains the work of the Holy Spirit as empowering each person into full humanity. As in the case of the autistic woman I mentioned previously. As she interacted with the Holy Spirit, she found peace in the most ambiguous situation one could imagine. She was mute, awkward, fidgety, and seemingly unfocused. And yet, she was aware not only that there was activity around her but what that activity was and what others were saying. Her communion with the Holy Spirit in those long decades of silence enabled and empowered her humanity. In a rare glimpse into the often incomprehensible and mysterious work of the Holy Spirit, she found communication later in life. Her willingness to share her experience allows those of us trapped in the noise and busyness of the typical world to catch a glimpse of God.

This glimpse of God invites us to consider the presence of God in our lives and in this world. In Romans 8, Paul writes of this vast relationship that begins for believers in Christ and extends to the world. Sin, weakness, suffering, revival, and reconciliation are all the realm of the Spirit. The Holy Spirit enters in to bring about movement for those who have remained idle far too long and to bring change for the dark places needing light. In this sense, the Holy Spirit is performing an illocutionary act speaking to individuals and communities about what it is that Scripture says and God

10. Yong, *Theology and Down Syndrome*, 181.

desires.[11] It is not necessarily an audible spoken word but it is palpable nonetheless. The Holy Spirit also cries out on our behalf when we have no words. If there were ever a community lacking the ability to adequately express all that is within, it is those who are unable to speak clearly for themselves, those who wonder why their own bodies betray them, those who know they are different but do not know what to do about it, those with perfectly functioning minds but with physical limitations that cause others to treat them as inferior, those who long to participate but require an able bodied person to slow down to get to know them and their ways of communicating. It is the Holy Spirit who whispers or blows like a hurricane according to need. It is the Holy Spirit who is alive and active at this point in history when there is a concerted effort across traditions and across the world to live more Christianly as we seek to best embrace and move beyond welcome for all friends, families, and those directly impacted by disability.

Questions for Reflection and Ministry Application

1. Is the Holy Spirit hindered or helped by intellectual disability?

2. Jesus was the disabled God who endured suffering, severe limitation, mocking, stares, embarrassment, and was seen as cursed. How might this encourage someone with a disability? And someone seemingly without a disability?

3. In light of the value from God of each member of his creation, how should this affect our faith communities when we gather? What would need to go and what would need to be added?

11. For more on the illocutionary act of the Holy Spirit see Grenz, "How Do We Know What to Believe?," 23.

3

SOVEREIGNTY
Who's in charge here?

"For voice is the process of articulating the world from a distinctive embodied position."—Nick Couldry

A T CAMP, LATE NIGHTS, early mornings, and close proximity create an environment where words just spill out more freely than elsewhere. So, naturally, it was at camp that I heard a young man say what I had always suspected many felt. He uttered the words, "I'm just a waste of space." It was said out loud in a moment of utter frustration and vulnerability. You could see him regret it as soon as we all heard him. It was only day two of camp. He had four more days with our group and then a full day's drive to get back home. The group went silent for a few seconds. Then, the Holy Spirit blew through our midst. There was a mixture of encouragement for this young man, "Mark," as he looked down, embarrassed that those words had slipped through his lips while others confessed that they, too, felt just like that.

Knowing a little about the context of this statement helps. Mark was shorter than his peers; and by shorter, I mean he was three-foot-something when he was told he was finished growing. He was a junior in high school and often offered up any joke that might have been aimed at him before anyone else could even think of it. He used humor as a defense mechanism and it had served him well over the years. Our camp team was at the challenge course on this particular day and before us stood "the wall." It was flat and nearly ten feet tall. The goal was to get the entire team over the wall, no one was to be left behind. Mark just couldn't see how he could be a part of this activity. I didn't yet know very much about working with teenagers, let alone teens with any special needs. It never crossed my mind that this particular element would be a problem. Later I learned Mark knew it was coming up and had been dreading our time at the wall. In fact, he had been so focused on it he didn't sleep well at camp and missed out on a few things the previous day.

We were focused on trying to figure out how to get everyone over the wall. This included a series of options like having the tallest person jump for the top, making a pyramid for some to climb, dangling one person by the legs for the rest of the team to climb, and a host of other options. In each case, the conversation always included what to do with Mark. Mark became the problem, the burden to bear for the group. It was as unintentional as it was clear. This clarity is what made the unintentionality immaterial. Mark couldn't joke his way out of this one and the weight of the time figuring out what to do came crashing down on him.

While Mark said the words, "I feel like a waste of space," it resonated with the other teens. Their struggles may not have been as obvious, but this sentiment summed up how they too felt. I've had this conversation with many youth leaders and camp staff since meeting Mark and there is a remarkable universality to this sentiment. For some it is pervasive. For others it is only in particular settings. The conversation that week of camp and in hundreds of talks since then always returns to the question of God as sovereign creator. In other words, did God really know what he was doing? People begin to wonder, "for all that is beautiful and good in creation, am I the exception? Am I a mistake?"

Sovereign Creator—I am not a mistake

This question of whether any person is a mistake demands a look at the doctrine of the sovereignty of God. Sovereignty leads to discussions and ponderings of would God, could God have chosen something different? It is a conversation for those who are weighed down by the supposition of what is and what is not worthy in the world. When it comes to debilitating, pervasive, and life-altering disability, one can wonder just what happened and where God is. The world values and favors able bodies and able minds. Assuming that God actually had even a modicum of control in the creation and establishment of this world, it is easy to see how the very sovereignty of God could be called into question. To make matters worse, sovereignty is one of those theological spaces that can be tricky as it has just as often been used as a weapon as a point of encouragement and hope.

In simplest form, sovereignty is accepting that "God alone has the prerogative to declare what his creation should be."[1] While God creates according to his own prerogative, God cannot create that which is contrary to his own character. At the core, God is love, and love is good. Consequently, as Tillich states so simply, "creation is good in its essential character."[2] God's free act of creation is not done out of necessity. God is complete in Godself, God is love and this is complete within the Trinity apart from creation. Consequently, this free act of creation that is non-necessary and non-compulsory is able to flow from love, not in need of love.[3] God's very act of love gives way to creation over and over again as an expression of goodness. Paul Tillich declared this decades ago simply stating "creation is good in its essential character."[4] Creation is good. There is nothing that is created that is not good. There are no mistakes, there is no waste of space. As created, each and every bit of creation is good! As God creates now, just as in Genesis, there is a declaration that it is good!

If only we could stop with the comment that creation is good. We see so much in this world that makes such a statement problematic, at least on the surface. Tillich, while stating plainly that all creation is good, is quick to offer that upon the heels of the very moment of creation comes actualization and with actualization comes estrangement from God. While holding a firm belief that the essential nature is good, Tillich also believes that if creation is "actualized, it falls into universal estrangement through freedom and destiny."[5] Ian Markham offers a helpful conversation and distinction disentangling what Tillich seems to intertwine. He argues that "The creating, sustaining, and goodness of the creation are truths which are logically prior to our growth and rebellion against the creator . . . our existence is good, while our inevitable growth and rebellion is harder to cope with."[6] Declaring creation as good is not to bury our heads in the sand and pretend sin does not exist. The converse is also true, declaring that sin exists neither undermines nor negates the fact that creation is good— creation, all creation, every single last one of us is good. And we enter a

---

1. Grenz, *Theology for the Community of God*, 139.

2. Tillich, *Systematic Theology*, vol. 2, 43.

3. Grenz, *Theology for the Community of God*, 130.

4. Tillich, *Systematic Theology*, vol. 2, 44.

5. Ibid., 44.

6. Markham, *Understanding Christian Doctrine*, 115.

sinful, fragmented, broken world where God is already present and about the work of reconciliation.

Understanding creation as good is primary in accepting God as good. I have lost count of the number of young adults who have said on hard days that they know God is good but surely *they* somehow were the exception to God's good creation. In other words, they felt like a mistake. It is understandable why this notion has been passed down and erroneously accepted in the church. This notion is due primarily to Augustine. Augustine saw the very act of the creation of a child as sinful as well as the actual child! Augustine popularized the notion that "a baby is getting the just consequence of being born into sin. A baby mysteriously participated in the sin of Adam and by virtue of that act is justly condemned to hell."[7] This notion that a baby, any baby born is so bad that it ought to be condemned to hell cannot be overstated in its impact on the doctrine of creation. That said, it either undermines God's role in creation as God is good and the baby is not, therefore God no longer has anything to do with creation. Or it posits that what God creates is so flawed its only justifiable destiny is hell, which calls into questions the core characteristic of God being good. Neither of these is possible. Consequently it is impossible for God to create anyone who is less than good. There are no mistakes.

So what do we make of the oppressive sense that some have accepted that some of us are, if not mistakes, then substandard—inferior. Nothing could be more contrary to character of God. Everyone is created in the image of God and holds equal value. People with disabilities struggle with the same insecurities and doubts we all have, but with the added pressure of a world that favors those who are cognitively and physically typical. They are mocked, teased, treated as mascots, and abused. That is before we have even noted the places where the church has been less than welcoming over the centuries. This manner of oppression ought not exist, but it does. "The reality of evil calls into question the affirmation of God's care over his creation . . . . Because evil appears to be on the rampage while the righteous suffer, it seems that God is not ordering the affairs of the world . . . . God is directing human affairs to the final revelation of his sovereignty and the reordering of the universe in the new heaven and the new earth . . . . And even now he invites us to orient our lives around his on-going program."[8] Oppression is not God's design. It is a twisting of what was intended and

7. Ibid., 107.

8. Grenz, *Theology for the Community of God*, 160–61.

God is constantly at work to right that perversion. Jesus spent his entire adult life reversing the understanding of power, privilege, and belonging. God cares deeply for those pushed aside and left at the margins, so much so that that is where Jesus hung out. As followers of Jesus, we get to lean into his sovereignty and it reverses the hierarchy that reigns in our world, marginalizing those with disabilities.[9]

The Trinity models for believers the beauty of relationship. "Because God is the Trinitarian community of love, God need not create the world to actualize his character. Yet because God is love his creation of the world is fully in keeping with his character."[10] God didn't need to create to find love—rather it was because God is love that creation took place. What is also important is understanding that the Trinity is a community of love. God is a god of relationships, within the Trinity, and, importantly, with God's creation. This is by design. It would behoove believers then to follow this same pattern of God in relationship as we approach those with disabilities. In other words, it is a relationship. It is not philanthropy or charity work, but a reciprocal relationship that constitutes true friendship. How can one capable of true friendship be a mistake? Amos Yong unpacks this further, writing of what it means to be known in mutually valuable ways and not as a mistake. There is mutual value, both in giving and receiving friendship.[11] Friendship is one of the many clues we have that those with disabilities are not mistakes.

God's sovereignty can be a hard pill to swallow when we declare that all are created equal and valued, yet experience a very different reality every day. It is clear that much of what takes place in the world around us is impacted by sin and is far from what God desires. How then do we reconcile God's sovereignty with a world so hurtful and harmful to those with disabilities? Stanley Grenz offers this helpful explanation.

> God's present sovereignty means that the present situation is connected to the future fullness. If God is sovereign at the end of history, then all history is moving toward the great day when God acts in a final manner to bring creation to completion. Because

9. Donald Kraybill wrote a wonderful book on the reversal of hierarchy back in 1978. While Kraybill's book is not about disability, it speaks clearly to the concerns of all marginalization. It was written at a time when disability rights were being addressed by activists on the margins of society. The Western church however was largely unaware of the shift to come. See Kraybill, *The Upside Down Kingdom*.

10. Grenz, *Theology for the Community of God*, 133.

11. Yong, *Theology and Down Syndrome*, 186-87.

our present moment is a point along the path en route to the day of God's eschatological sovereignty, it too participates in the movement of history through which God is directing human affairs toward the accomplishment of his goal.[12]

Grenz offers the terms *de jure* (by right or by law) and *de facto* (what actually is) as ways to unpack this sovereignty. God is sovereign *de facto* in the moments when we are in accordance with his plans. This is a part of our free will and glimpses of what God intends here on earth as it is in heaven. This, unfortunately, is not as common as believers would like. A lack of seeing things as God intended does not negate God's sovereignty. Rather, it orients God's sovereignty to history knowing that the eternal God will have his sovereignty revealed in the end. We know that "God's human creatures do not always love in accordance with his design or will for them. Insofar as we are not what God intends us to be nor do what God intends that we do, God is not now de facto sovereign. Yet, this is not the end of the story. At the eschaton God will bring all creation into conformity with the divine design. Then he will not only be sovereign de jure but also de facto."[13] For those with disabilities, the pain, sorrow, and suffering will be reversed. It may not happen in the timing we would like but we are called to work for it still. God's *de jure* sovereignty is the hope and promise that draws believers to seek *de facto* sovereignty here and now. For those with disabilities who wonder if God is in control, the answer is yes. It may not look like it yet, but "God always acts in accordance with his own character, which is love."[14] This love reminds us that there is no one who is a mistake, no one who is beyond God's compassion, no one who does not have all they need to be in the eternal presence in a place of honor for all eternity.

Questions for Reflection and Ministry Application

1. How does your view of God's sovereignty influence your understanding of someone with a disability?

2. Have you ever considered in what ways you fall short or are disabled in some manner? How does your self-awareness of these fit into your understanding of God's sovereignty?

12. Grenz, *Theology for the Community of God*, 141–42.

13. Ibid.

14. Ibid., 139.

4

THEOLOGICAL ANTHROPOLOGY

What does it mean to be human?

"We don't see things as they are, we see them as we are."
—Anais Nin

Nick Palermo is a man who has worked in ministry with teens and families impacted by disability for more than thirty years. He is the founder of Young Life's Capernaum ministry and Emmaus ministry. He tells the following story about what it means to be human.

One of my favorite moments with teens is welcoming them to youth group. I love the first time looking directly into their eyes and repeating their name back to them during the introduction. I love to tell them how glad I am that they are here. Some light up with a huge smile, others are more shy and look to the floor or cling like a small child to the individual who is introducing them. It's my favorite moment because I know the adventure that is in store for them—that from this moment on, their life will be changed.

On one particular day, I was expecting to meet someone new. As I joined our team of volunteers in picking up kids after school, I scanned the eagerly awaiting crowd for a new face. They all looked familiar as we began loading up the vans. A few minutes later a teacher came out of her classroom escorting a tall young woman with light brown hair—the new girl I was expecting. They walked slowly and deliberately. "This is Susie," the teacher announced. I looked into her eyes and said warmly, "Hi, Susie." No response. Instinctively, I suspected that Susie was autistic. A common misconception about individuals with autism is that nothing gets through to them. In reality it is just the opposite. Everything gets through to them as if the volume were set to ten. The effect is that an autistic person shuts down to filter out the overwhelming stimulation coming in through their senses.

So reading Susie was next to impossible over the next few weeks as she continued to join us. Was she having a good time? Did she like being there? What was going on in her private world? Many times Susie would stand and gently rock herself with a blank expression. I would look hoping to see what was going on behind her sherry-colored eyes, but I could discern nothing. I longed to make some type of connection with her. When I touched her hand to lead her to sit down, she would pull it back as if it had been burned. In spite of this apparent lack of connection to anyone during youth group, she continued to come week after week.

That summer, surprisingly, Susie signed up for camp. In order to attend, she would need someone to be with her around the clock. A wonderful high school sophomore named Ashley volunteered to be Susie's guide, friend, and attendant for the week. Ashley had been to camp earlier that summer and had given her life to Christ. She jumped at the opportunity to give back out of her new relationship with him and others. It would be a costly, sacrificial act of service and kindness. There would be very little free time, if any. Ashley would have to attend to Susie's every need. She would be responsible to help her integrate into the life of the camp, meet other kids who would likely be afraid of and avoid her. She would have to help her eat, dress, and take her to the restroom. Ashley would be Susie's secure point of contact in a frightening and unknown world.

The middle of the week brought a Western hoedown. Susie let Ashley lead her in dancing. She followed Ashley and the rest of the campers and seemed to be connecting with the joy and movement of dance. As the dance ended Ashley led Susie over to the basketball bleachers to rest along with two other leaders, Lydia and Shelley. Caught up in the fun spirit of the evening, I headed over to join them. When I reached them, I broke out into a spontaneous silly dance while singing at the top of my lungs. Shelley interrupted me and whispered, "Nick, look at Susie." I turned and witnessed a wonder—a God moment. Susie was rocking herself, but instead of staring vacantly, both sides of her mouth were curled up in a smile. Her eyes were sparkling with silent mirth as she was looking at me. I was caught completely off guard and stood speechless, smiling right back. Inwardly, I was overcome with awe. It appeared to be an ordinary and insignificant moment, but I knew I stood in the presence of God who lived behind Susie's eyes and for that instant had brought her out to play.

I look at Susie and know there is a God wildly in love with her. A God who created her, not as an accident, but in his image. A God faithful to her. A God who delights to use the "nobodies" of this world to shame the "somebodies." Susie, a very ordinary, cracked clay jar through which the light of Christ spills out. I cannot wait for that day in heaven when Susie's voice is loosed and she is healed. I plan to sit down with her and have a very long conversation. But first I'll do a silly little dance in front of her to hear the sound of her laughter. I think she'll say, "Sit down. I have a lot to tell you."

Theological Anthropology

The story of Susie is a story about theological anthropology. It is the story of a young woman who was not seen, until she was. This is the story of many people with disabilities. They are invisible to much of the world. When they are seen, they are too often a problem to solve rather than a person to celebrate. This is a blind spot in most of our churches. Blind spots are a normal part of life. We all have them. We often miss what is right in front of us. There is a famous video about visual perception where the instructions are to count how many times a team wearing white shirts passes a basketball. The team in white is playing in the midst of a team dressed in black shirts. The crazy part is that in the middle of all of this playing, a full-sized person in a gorilla suit dances through the game. It is surprisingly common to have an entire group watch this video and miss the gorilla. It is not that they weren't looking; they just weren't looking for the gorilla.[1] Most of us approach the world with a set of expectations similar to what we have already experienced. This is perfectly understandable. We learn through life experience and each experience adds to our repertoire of what we believe we can reasonably expect in the future. This goes for personal interaction as well. We are surprised when someone cuts us off in speaking when we have been socialized to take turns. We are uncomfortable when someone stands too close and doesn't recognize the invisible, yet very real, personal bubble. Each of our lives is filled with a set of expectations, verified by experience that reinforces what we hold dear. Experiences that deviate from

---

1. To check out this video on your own, see http://www.youtube.com/watch?v=vJG698U2Mvo or go to You Tube and search "Selective Attention Test." Of course, you now know to look for the gorilla and it will seem obvious.

our expectations may jar us temporarily but do not often bring a shift in our future expectations unless they are particularly poignant.

Almost fifty years ago, two dedicated scientists, Arno Penzias and Robert Wilson, set out to use a high-powered radio telescope in order to map sections of the Milky Way that appear to be devoid of stars. What they expected and what they saw, or rather heard, were two very different things. Their research hypothesis had them focus on seeking faint echoes that would allow for this mapping. What they heard was a static noise that simply could not be explained away. In defeat, after a year of listening to static, they called a colleague to see if he had any ideas about where they had gone wrong. Much to their surprise, he declared that they had not gone wrong. They had found what others were seeking. Penzias and Wilson simply had not been able to hear the evidence they sought due to their expectations suggesting they should hear something else. They had missed what was right in front of them. They thought it was an anomaly, a mistake, or simply in the way of what they were really hoping to find. Thanks to the conversation with another scientist, someone with a different perspective, they were able to truly hear what had been in front of them all along. Because of their discovery, in 1978, they won the Nobel Prize for physics.[2]

So what do gorillas and scientists have to do with a theological understanding of people? More than you might imagine. Similar to the scientists, most of us need to be encouraged to listen differently. If we take the time to listen, voices from the marginalized edges of society are not only present, they are deafening. They can be missed, blending in with the white noise of our world. Yet their voices are there, clear and present. There are many arguments regarding stem cell research, at what point life begins, eugenics, and a host of other issues all swirling around notion of the human.[3] When we slow down enough, we are able to differentiate the voices from the mix of noise in our world. Perhaps, we would begin to recognize, really recognize, as human those who have been categorized as less than human, less than the image of God. Jean Vanier is the founder of L'Arche, a ministry where typically abled and non-typically abled people agree to live with one another as family. He writes and speaks all over the world. He describes his experience as follows. "I go into schools and I hear kids saying, 'If I have a monster within me, I will get rid of it.' That reality is there. Of course, if the mother sees the child as a terrible disappointment, then the child feels

2. Lehrer, "Accept Defeat."
3. Hauerwas and Vanier, Living Gently, 69.

that he or she is a disappointment .... Deep down the self-image of the child is broken. The child feels 'I am no good.' The heart of L'Arche is to say to people, 'I am glad you exist.'"[4] It is not only the heart of L'Arche, but the heart of God that states, "I am glad you exist!" But God also states, "I created you and declared that you are good!" For far too long Christian history remained silent or condemned those with disabilities.[5] That is not the task at hand but it does bear weight on what takes place in this book. My presupposition is that all people (regardless of physical or mental ability) are human. But what exactly does it mean to be human?

Theological anthropology offers the grounds for conversation into which we are forced when we wrestle with what it means to be human. The Christian understanding of human carries with it the connotation of being created in the image of God. Let me stipulate that God is perfect, holy, and other and that humankind was made in God's image. What then does it mean for humans to declare any person with disabilities to be categorically different? To be atypical? Such a declaration begs the question of the definition of typical. There are, of course, differences between the typically and differently abled. Still, it is far more common to hear the differences between us articulated than our similarities. How far can different go until different is wholly other? This is the question at hand.

We need to back up and look at an arc of theological anthropology. Its precedence is neither historical nor biblical. The notion of wrestling with the concept of humanity for early Christians was practically unthinkable, given cultural and time constraints. With very little free time apart from work for survival, contemplation was focused on who God was, not who we are. In fact, Scripture has no dedicated book on this topic, yet there is mention of the essence, position, and desired interaction of humans both to God and one another. Genesis 1:26–30 gives humans a glimpses into their place in the world. We are created in God's image and likeness. This writing was a reversal of the Israelite tradition as expressed in Ezekiel 1:26 where the prophet describes the likeness of God as being like the appearance of a human.[6] Still, an anthropocentric doctrine exists and errs too much on the side of humanity, neglecting the rightful position of God. It reduces God to human terms rather than magnifying the human in divine terms.[7] Humans

---

4. Ibid., 69.

5. For a more detailed account of this see Yong, *Theology and Down Syndrome*, 19–42.

6. Smith, *The Origins of Biblical Monotheism*, 90.

7. Ibid., 90.

are given a place of honor, distinction, and responsibility eclipsed only by that of the angelic host as seen in Psalm 8:3–9 and Hebrews 2:5–13. And yet, theological anthropology does come into being and in some cases, becomes a central tenet. Origen, Augustine, and Aquinas all hold discussion regarding the createdness of humanity. In contradistinction to Gnostics, this affirmed God as Creator as much as it spoke of those created.

Just how does one prevent the reduction of God in light of the magnification of humanity? Tertullian affirmed "that the doctrine of the Trinity was to be divinely revealed, not humanly constructed."[8] It is in this divine revelation that we look for an understanding of God. One place that God's self-revelation comes through is the *imago dei*. Genesis 1:26–30 offers particular insight as God created male and female (plural). God's own image demands unity in plurality.[9] This unity in plurality draws attention toward the very particularities which comprise the unity.

The particularities of the Trinity must be addressed not as separation, modalism, or tritheism. As people, we too often pathologize particularities, we view them as diseased or aberrant. In turn we do the same to God. This results in pathologizing one or the other members of the Godhead as subordinate to the other members of the Trinity or as less than deity entirely. Rejecting the fragmentation of particularities, we prevent pathologizing and instead conceive of God trinitarianly.[10] As we embrace the Trinity, we may also conceive of those created in his image in all their particularities. It is the Trinity that requires us to look at intersectionality not as a problem, but as created by design.

Createdness implies that indeed there is a creation. Modernity ushered in a look at context. The former hermeneutical approach sought objectivity, which not only elevated ignoring condition but denied its very existence. This was seen as an improvement over the denial of the particularities of those who had been created. Eleazar Fernandez reminds us that "this hermeneutic move toward conditionedness points in the proper direction, but the move has been aborted and left hanging before it has touched the ground."[11] What is meant by conditionedness here includes our physical bodies. Objectivity (if there is such a thing) required a separation of body

---

8. Erickson, *Christian Theology*, 342.

9. Ibid., 329; Jewett, *Man as Male and Female*, 33–40, 43–48; Barth, *Church Dogmatics*, vol. 3, part 1, 183–201.

10. Gunton, *The One, the Three and the Many*, 177.

11. Fernandez, *Reimagining the Human*, 12.

and knowing. The body is to be separated so as to not bias or influence knowing. But separation is not possible. Our body, our context is unavoidable. "Context is not merely the space that is the recipient of my actions; it is also that which shapes who we are and how we see things around us."[12] The move, using a disembodied knowledge, has been criticized heavily by those who consider marginalized communities. We are not all identical and it is folly to think so. "Embodied knowing sees reality through the configuration of our bodiliness and seriously considers the effects of ideas as they bear on bodies and vice versa, especially the disfigured bodies of the marginalized."[13] For generations, a disfigured body has been seen as flawed and undesirable. When considered in context, Jesus Christ himself lived through disfigurement and when raised from the dead, still bore those scars. It is time to embrace both types of bodies, those defined by society as desirable and those considered disfigured. Since disfigured bodies bear similarities to Christ's resurrected body, they are equally desirable by God.

Modernity poses another difficulty when considering our initial question of what it means to be human. It assumes that "the self emerges either through mastery of nature viewed as external to the self or through mastery of the inner realm so that the self may reflect some supposedly universal human essence."[14] But what happens when your body betrays you and mastery of the external and inner realm are no longer options? Is mastery required to be human? Revisiting Psalm 8, Jim McClendon states that "mortal stewardship is not determined by partitioning human nature off from the rest of nature."[15] In fact, he goes on to write that the remaining task of theological anthropology is to point toward "a view of creation that can replace the old human rulership and mastery views that have shown themselves so disposed to corruption."[16] Being human is not about what we can or cannot master. It is about being created in the image of God. Being created in the image of God solves the issue of mastery but it still does not define the image of God. Rather, it raises the question. Too often we assume the image of God will bear a striking resemblance to what we deem as acceptable and right. It is to this task we must now turn.

---

12. Ibid., 24.

13. Ibid., 13.

14. Grenz, *The Social God and the Relational Self*, 98.

15. McClendon, *Doctrine: Systematic Theology*, vol. 2, 157.

16. Ibid.

The image orthodox Christianity holds dear is a communal God. It is impossible to even approach a definition of God apart from community. What I mean by this is both the community of the Trinity and the realized and invisible community of the church. God is a communal being, as the Father, Son, and Holy Spirit being the Creator, Redeemer, and Sustainer. From what we have considered thus far, theological anthropology is firmly oriented around the *imago dei* as impacted by Trinitarian theology.[17] To be created in the image of God is to be communal. To be communal is to be recognized by others and in relation with others. It is more than a Kantian I-Thou, as it embraces a reciprocal socialization. You cannot be in my presence and remain the same and I cannot be in your presence and remain the same. There is a mutual impact occurring. Realistically, community is most often built primarily upon what we find in common. This can be food, hobbies, education, or a variety of life occurrences. There are times this is a natural occurrence and other times that this is an intentional interaction. Intentional interactions occur when an awareness has been raised and an individual or group works to bring seemingly unlike people together. This can be a youth group regularly visiting a nursing home or a professional sports team visiting local schools. Another possibility exists. When two disparate groups, who on the surface seem wholly other, find commonality transcending those differences, the groups can begin to see one another as *holy* other. This occurs most often through circumstances that are not of our choosing. You may relate to others who have lost a child to death, who share an illness or find themselves in dire financial straits, or worse. Any three of these options may change your community to include those with disabilities.

We are incomplete without those who differ from us. Our view of God also is incomplete without the earnest presence and dialogue with voices (audible and inaudible) that differ from our own. "They are necessary because it is only through the frail instrumentality of another that we can be liberated from the regimes of truth that we create, and necessary because it is only through conspiracy and companionship that we gain the power to dismantle and construct alternative ways of thinking and dwelling."[18] Our communities give context to shape and be shaped by our interactions as we live in the image of God as humans. No mastery is required and each person is lifted up with the growth of a Trinitarian focus of theological

17. Grenz, *The Social God and the Relational Self*, 223.

18. Fernandez, *Reimagining the Human*, 27.

anthropology. We need each other to point out what has always been before us but hidden away, literally and figuratively.

Questions for Reflection and Ministry Application

1. What do you think it means to be human in light of this chapter? What are basic human rights? Needs?

2. Which point addressed in this chapter has challenged your way of viewing what it means to be created in the image of God the most? Why?

3. Embodied particularities are often pointed out for how individuals do not fit in. In what ways might you be able to now address non-typical development as being a reflection of God rather than an anomaly or distortion of God?

5

SIN

Who or what is broken?

"Deep down in human existence there is an experience of seeing the light and turning away from it, either because it is too beautiful to behold or because it spoils the dank but familiar darkness. Deep down in human existence there is an experience of reaching for forbidden fruit, of pushing away loving arms, of breaking something on purpose just to prove that you can. Deep down in human existence there is an experience of doing whatever is necessary to feed and comfort the self, because there is no one else to trust, no other purpose to serve, no other god to follow."—Barbara Brown Taylor

Individual

SITTING ON A CABIN floor with fifteen girls with disabilities packed in, the topic of sin arose. I asked the girls what they thought the word *sin* meant, not really expecting a long conversation. It turned into a conversation that lasted the rest of the week. It was a conversation that took place in large groups and individually. There was the typical teenage girl drama of gossiping about a friend, knowing they were disrespecting a teacher, going too far sexually, or playing up their disability to get something they wanted from strangers. A few were even honest enough to say they wished they had a chance to come home late or get caught smoking or some other forbidden activity. As they were always chaperoned some said they had never really *done* anything wrong. It turned out the boys were having similar discussions in their cabins as well.

What struck me was not the open conversations from these girls but a comment by a new leader trying to process the conversation. She wondered if these girls were given a special pass for sin as compensation for the hardships they endured due to disability. I could understand her compassion in this comment, but realized she had a fundamental misunderstanding of sin. She saw sin as a transactional encounter or action in which someone volitionally does something wrong, such as getting drunk or driving too fast, and a consequence follows. As most of our girls did not even have access to these kinds of opportunities to "sin," her thought was that surely sin was not a part of their worlds. I didn't fully know how to respond at the time. What I did know was that recognizing both that sin impacts those with disabilities and that they are capable of sin was important. More than merely important, it is imperative that we avoid conceptualizing a special dispensation for those with disabilities concerning sin if we are to take seriously that those with disabilities are just as human as anyone else.

Sin, then, must be understood more robustly than simply missing the mark. That said, the missing-the-mark metaphor cannot be ignored due to its impact on our theology of sin and a modest measure of explanatory power. Missing the mark is, perhaps, the most common understanding of sin. It is the phrase frequently used to translate the Hebrew verb חטא (chata) and the Greek verb ἁμαρτάνω (hamartano). "Missing the mark" moves us beyond seeing sin as just making mistakes and more fully expresses that this is a volitional choice not to do what is right. It means that there is culpability in the action.[1] "Missing the mark" clearly names both the action and the result of the action as being counter to what God intends. It is the stuff of great sermons. It draws us to reflection and repentance. The illustration is so clear. There is a target with a bull's-eye. The bow is drawn and the archer does not aim well so that the arrow misses the center entirely. But the metaphor breaks down—as all metaphors do. The trouble comes when the link between action and result are not clear or when drawing back and aiming at the center is too difficult or impossible for a variety of reasons. If "missing the mark" were the only understanding of sin, then it would be in keeping with God's characteristic love to extend special dispensation for those who simply cannot aim well.

Neither is all sin merely about running around wreaking havoc, harming self or others. Our understanding of sin must also include the Hebrew term עָוָה (*'awah*) which is translated into English as "to bend, or be

---

1. Erickson, *Christian Theology*, 567.

bent, to twist, or bowed down."[2] Rather than brash, bold actions unleashed upon the world, this understanding of sin includes a closing in, a perversion of what was supposed to be.[3] This type of sin can be seen when someone becomes so self-absorbed with their very existence and struggles that they are kept from being all that God has created them to be. This type of sin can paralyze and consume the sinner with self-doubt that leads to self-loathing and prevents living life as God desires and serving others as God directs. Grenz explains, "If our divinely given design is that we be God's image bearer, we must understand sin as our failure to reflect the image of God."[4] Picture a person hunched over, living in a world that has made her the center of all thought and action. While persons with disability are often ignored and marginalized, their families, conversely, run the risk of making them the center of their worlds. They become the lens through which every decision is made. Placing a person with a disability in this central position, even unknowingly, constitutes idolatry, dethroning God, replacing him with self or the loved one who has a disability. At times, it is a personal choice (individual)—if the person with a disability lives into this role—and, at other times, this position has been foisted upon them by friends or the outside world (social).[5] When our first daughter was born, she was born with a ventricular septal defect. Three holes in her heart came with a host of complications and required around-the-clock attention. Very early on, our pediatrician cautioned us to not make her the identified patient of our family or she would live into that role. For many people with disabilities, being the center of their own world has been a learned behavior that they

2. Ibid., 574.

3. I am grateful to one of my professors, Dr. Millard Erickson, for so many reasons. His explanation of 'awah is incredibly helpful. I, however, want to make clear that in no way is the connection between sin and the presence of a disability necessarily a perversion of what was intended. There are times when a disability is clearly a result of sin such as impaired cognition in the life of a person born with fetal alcohol syndrome. There are also times when there is no volitional action that could have created or prevented a particular disability. See the previous section on the sovereignty of God for a discussion on the existence of disability not as punishment but as reality.

4. Grenz, *Theology for the Community of God*, 242.

5. Several years ago I did a research project where I interviewed families regarding their experience with youth ministry and their children with disabilities. One couple in particular had a comment that has stayed with me. They said that for many if not most of their friends, their child became the center of their world. They saw marriages, siblings, and lives shipwrecked with the best of intentions behind family choices. They however were committed to Christ being the center of their world and their daughter with a disability was a vibrant, vital part of that world but not the center.

are the only ones who matter. All meals, all travel, all conversation, and all existence in the family centers around them. It is a self-involved, myopic existence that is incredibly difficult to change.

Conceptualizing sin as both "missing the mark" and "being bent or twisted inward" can be both a humbling and liberating occurrence. It is exhausting to focus solely on oneself and never others. It is a posture of always being on and never having something to contribute. What can begin as care and nurture, holds a person in captivity as "the needy one." John Swinton draws out the work of Reynolds and Creamer noting that we *all* start life as dependent and vulnerable. It is natural. When we are dependent and vulnerable, we open ourselves to struggles: rejection, exploitation, and loneliness; as well as possibilities: welcome, care, and love.[6] All infants are in need of constant care and, in healthy situations, their very existence is a gift back to the family. As the infant grows into childhood, adolescence, and adulthood, care is still needed. If, however, that care is not developmentally and individually appropriate, struggles continue and possibilities disappear. That person can remain captive to the caregiver, never being allowed to contribute to others in any way. This has too often been the situation for those with disabilities. When few or no opportunities are given, it is no wonder that a person lives into the role of being the center of their own world. Realizing the place of God in their lives, liberation follows as their eyes are lifted, shifting the focus from themselves to Jesus. This shift opens the possibility of mutually welcoming each other into their lives for vulnerability and possibility. Being in relationship becomes as much about what one may give as what one receives. No longer is any individual the center of the world. Christ is. With this perspective we may serve one another as we would serve Christ.

Many people with disabilities understand the consequences of sin long before they understand sin itself. They are ignored, ridiculed, mocked, and isolated. They are sinned upon and can feel broken inside. They deal with sin. There is no need to convince them of its existence. The point of this section is not to further harm or blame those with disabilities. It is to make clear that sin is a reality in their lives, just as it is in the lives of all human beings. When the reality of sin is named, it may be addressed. "Sin is our only hope because the recognition that something is wrong is the first step toward setting it right again. There is no help for those who admit needing no help. There is no repair for those who insist nothing is broken, and there

---

6. Swinton, "Disability, Ableism, and Disablism," 447.

is no hope of transformation for a world whose inhabitants accept that it is sadly but irreversibly wrecked."[7] Not naming sin allows it to continue to be present, to grow, and prevent those with disabilities from being in full fellowship with God and others. In naming sin we may then also address the result of sin, isolation from God and/or others. The privilege we have in the work Christ did on the cross is that isolation, in particular, the acute isolation from God, is not inevitable.

Corporate

Having established sin as being a combination of missing the mark and being too self-focused, a brief discussion on its corporate impact is warranted. Already established in the section on sovereignty is the reality that disability is not necessarily a result of sin. That said, this notion has been present in our world and importantly in our churches and systems of belief from early on. In fact, the church has often justified the maltreatment of those with disabilities. In so many ways, it seems ridiculous and farfetched in today's world. And then, just as quickly, history repeats itself and stark reminders are given for why this conversation must not only continue but move forward. As early as the first and second centuries CE, Darrell Amundsen notes, "it can be categorically asserted that there were no laws in classical antiquity, Greek or Roman, that prohibited the killing, by exposure or otherwise, of the defective newborn."[8] Importantly this quote was included in a chapter by Almut Caspary on the Patristic Era and early attitudes toward those with disabilities. She follows with this quote with the comment that "The reason for such a rejection of deformed newborn life seems to have been the negligibility of its contribution to the future public good."[9] This phrase "negligibility of its contribution to the future public good" interpreting attitudes and practices from the first and second centuries was echoed as late as 2014 by Richard Dawkins. He tweeted that the *only* ethical choice a pregnant woman has upon learning her fetus has Down Syndrome is to abort. Dawkins then followed this up with a lengthier response asserting that people with disabilities bring suffering for themselves and others.[10]

---

7. Taylor, *Speaking of Sin*, 41.

8. Amundsen, *Medicine, Society, and Faith,* 55.

9. Caspary, "The Patristic Era," 27.

10. Dawkins, "Abortion & Down Syndrome." Dawkins does state that while this is his position, he is in line with the majority of women in America and Europe based on data

Dawkins contends those with a disability are a liability on society.[11] In fact, he argues a similar position to that of the first and second century. Happiness for all involved as well as society in general would be negatively impacted, therefore it is actually a moral choice to abort a child with a disability to preserve the greater public good.

Martin Luther has a different take that is worth noting here. He famously suggested that a twelve-year-old boy be suffocated who was "presumably suffering from Prader-Willi Syndrome."[12] In all fairness, Martin Luther was also working from a perspective of medieval superstitions and likely assumed the boy was a changeling, one made in the image of the devil, rather than of God. Luther actually has a great deal written that was tremendously countercultural in his day and offers a great deal of dignity to those who would have been considered subordinate by society's standards. He held a very high view of creation that included those with disabilities. According to Luther, "What human beings are is hence not to be defined by their attributes, their disposition, but by the image that God has promised to bestow on them in Christ."[13] To not treat someone with dignity for being in the image of God would be sin. The struggle is real in the times of Luther. His understanding of Scripture demanded respect and care for all humans. The times in which he lived blinded him to seeing some people with disabilities as human.

The forces that lead to how we treat one another are complicated. For generations, misinformation and social stigma have created a fear based society based on the worthy and unworthy of the world. Richard Beck names this as sin. "Sin is often characterized by the forces of dehumanization. These forces may be subtle or shockingly brutal. But they all share a common core: the stratification of humanity along a divinity dimension with superior groups (defined as "my tribe") elevated over other ("outside") groups. These forces of dehumanization affect how we treat others (e.g., moral circle), how we select scapegoats, and how we choose who is worthy of love and affection."[14] Those with disabilities have been stratified and determined to be inferior by the greater society across time and cultures.

---

regarding abortion and the reason why it is chosen. He states that he is not arguing for eugenics but agreeing with the masses that it is a moral choice.

11. Jacober, "Church and the Unmaking of Violence."

12. Heuser, "The Human Condition," 185.

13. Ibid., 191.

14. Beck, *Unclean*, 122.

There have of course been pockets of acceptance and grace, but on the whole, the world is a place that devalues those needing extra time, care, attention, or help. Interestingly, these are the very kinds of people Jesus says we are to serve as if we were serving him. It is the role of the church to reject this stratification within her walls and to cry out for an elimination of stratification in all of society. "If the church looks on injustice without holy anger it allows the institution of redemptive love to give shelter to loveless-ness, and is itself involved in the charge of hypocrisy."[15] The church must be at the forefront of speaking out for those with disabilities lest we give way to the forces of sin and lose our prophetic voice altogether.

Questions for Reflection and Ministry Application

1. Interact with this statement: the silence of the German Church in the 1930s with regards to Nazi policies contributed to the ability of the Holocaust to take place. In our present-day church, what ways are we being silent that could lead to future harm for those with disabilities?

2. How would you present sin to someone with a disability; physical, emotional, or cognitive? Moderate or severe?

15. Rauschenbusch, *Dare We Be Christians?*, 35.

6 _____

ECCLESIOLOGY
Who's missing?

"Enter the site of your tent, and let the curtains of your habitations stretch out."—Isaiah 54:2

A LITTLE OVER A DECADE ago I was working on a large research project where I simply asked families with a child with a disability to share their church experience. Overwhelmingly, the experiences were negative. I opened every interview with the same neutral question, "what is your experience with church?" One mother offered this response, "So I tried to look and every church I called, I asked 'is there a place for a special needs child?' every year as he got older—ten, eleven—there was not one church that I found that had a place for special needs kids . . . . I could not believe with all of the programs we have for the poor and rehab for drugs and you get in trouble, criminals, there's places, there's rehab, but for someone with a disability in the church, there's nothing that would have a child with disabilities and stay connected and get taught about Jesus or anything spiritual."[1] Again and again I was told that families cherished the church, but once they had a child with a special need, they could no longer be involved. I heard stories of being asked to leave as their child was too disruptive. Others were told that no one was able to handle their child. For many, they experienced sitting in pews, working hard to "handle" their own child and no one came to say hello, let alone help. What all but a few had in common is that they felt unwelcomed in countless small ways. It wasn't that anyone told them out loud church was no place for a family impacted by disability, but that was the message they received loud and clear. At some point, they just got

_____

1. Jacober, "Ostensibly Welcome," 67.

too tired to keep trying and experience rejection and stress in a place that was established by God to allow us to bear one another's burdens.

Somewhere in the last ten years, the relationship between the church and those with disabilities began to shift. Today, there are many more churches with ministries for children, adolescents, and adults with special needs. There are even more churches who have created space for the integration of people with special needs into the life of the church. Still others are in process trying to live into the convictions they hold and wanting to include others well. Just this morning I was contacted by a former student who is church planting. She was writing to ask for information on how to include those with disabilities at the very foundation of their ministry. I've heard leaders talk about not being able to do church without a great musician, a gifted preacher, a building, or finances. This was the first time I have heard from a former student saying they just didn't feel like they could be church in the world today without being intentional that everyone was included. What these very conversations have done is shift the questions from "what can the church do for those with disabilities?" to "what is the church lacking when people with disabilities are missing?" I would argue the church is not fully the body of Christ when all followers of Jesus are not included. In other words, we are not whole as God intended.

So what is it that God intends? There are many ways to consider the concept of church and just what it has been, what it is, and what it ought to be. While there are many metaphors and descriptions of what constitutes church, what they all hold in common is that church is God's idea not ours and therefore special needs cannot be dismissed. The four traditional marks of the church—one, holy, catholic, and apostolic—are the uncontested winners in defining church. They are the baseline for Christian churches. But what then? Ian Markham identifies four aspects of the theme of church within the New Testament. These aspects create room for the intentional inclusion of those with disabilities. The first aspect is that the church is the people of God (1 Pet 2:9). The second aspect is the body of Christ (1 Cor 12:27). The third aspect is safeguarding and passing on the tradition of faith (1 Cor 15:3). The fourth aspect is that the church is a community that creates virtue (2 Cor 4:5 and Gal 3:28).[2]

---

2. Markham, *Understanding Christian Doctrine*, 159–60.

Church as the people of God (1 Pet 2:9, Lev 26:13, 2 Corinthians 6:16)

To be the people of God is simultaneously awesome and pedestrian. It is awesome in that it is worthy of awe. It can take one's breath away to think the creator of the universe knows the very number of hairs on my head (Luke 12:7), knows my moves and thoughts (Ps 139:2), knows how to calm me when I am spinning out of control (Phil 4:6–7). It is pedestrian because there are so many of us who are God's people. We forget that this is amazing and special. We get caught up in the daily and take for granted what it is to be God's people. That is, unless we are part of the community of people who are being told in subtle and not-so-subtle ways that we do not belong. This could apply to so many people throughout history for so many reasons: wrong sex, wrong ethnicity, wrong age, wrong family. In this way, those with disabilities join a great cloud of witnesses who were not always welcome by others but were always included by God.

Those with disabilities have always been included by God, even when the leaders within the movement didn't get it. I can't help but think of a mom whom I interviewed for the research mentioned above. When she spoke of her daughter with Down Syndrome, she described her daughter as a prayer warrior, always taking the time to intercede and cry out for the needs of others. Yet, they could not find a youth group that would create space for her daughter's different pace of life. She had been a consistent and strong member of the church, but eventually was unable to attend church. They belonged to the invisible church, but longed for a visible gathering of God's people. The church has been described for centuries in terms of the invisible and visible church, the hidden and the seen. For centuries, faithful families shared Christ with loved ones never able to be a part of the gathering of other believers on a regular basis. This family was and is as much a part of the covenantal community of God as any other persons. Yet our buildings, our liturgy, and even our very theology communicated that someone who was differently able was not welcome, or worse, was condemned. It was wrong then. It is wrong now. We need a clear and intentional way to discuss church that includes all who are known by God. We need this because we are not who we were intended to be as church when a part of our body is not present.

The church is the bride of Christ seeking to spur one another on to love and good deeds. She is powerful in ways that defy explanation. She is to serve and from this humble position has strength to change the world. And yet, over the centuries, this self-understanding of power and strength has been distorted, excluding members who rightfully belong. Somewhere along the way, the church bought into her own hype and stopped living as one who is loved and chose instead to put on the appearance of perfection by excluding the differently abled. As much as this must grieve God's heart, God still loves the church and has been calling her back to her true nature. Part of that true nature is to be exactly as she was created to be: strong, weak, perfect, flawed, and beautiful.

The Body of Christ (1 Cor 12:18–27)

First Corinthians 12:18–27 calls the church to her intended existence. We each have a place and a role. No one is more or less important than the other. As much as we say this within the context of the gathered community, the visible church, we rarely wrestle deeply with the implications. If we really lived as if we believed that every single believer was as vital as the next to the health of the church, changes would have to be made. McNair writes of the discomfort that inclusion of those with disabilities brings.

> People who are "typical" may fear the notion of seeing people who are atypical (due to impairments, social skill deficits, etc.) as their equals because of the demands equality might place on them. If you are not my equal, I may feel I needn't change. However, if you are my equal, and you experience devaluation from me, that implies that I am very wrong in my interactions with you. Disability ministry, like loving my neighbor, will cost me something.[3]

When we value those with disabilities as equals, we move beyond charity and into actual relationship. This is hard when we come with the baggage of years of separation, isolation, and fighting for our own belonging and legitimacy in the world. God, however, never asked us to fight or prove anything. God did call us to be his body, his hands and feet, the community of believers gathered to spur one another on to love and good deeds in the world around us. What Andrew Zirschky writes of teenagers could be applied to all people, including those with disabilities. "When teenagers who are convinced that their belonging is based upon performance encounter a community of social equality, they often are able to release their

3. McNair, "The Power," 96.

anxiety because they experience that their performance isn't the source of their belonging."[4] We belong because God designed each and every one of us as precious and valuable, as equals.

The people of God belong together, strong and weak in paradoxical relationship. The church is the *people* of God, not the *person* of God. We are the people when we are together, strong and weak, both included by design. Weakness and strength are only perceptions and often incorrect perceptions. Jeff McNair addresses this, saying, "when considering who would seem weaker, one might think of people with disabilities."[5] Looking further at the text, it is not a pitting of weak against strong, it is a strong admonishment that both are needed. Those who seem weak are just as necessary as those who are strong. "Paul says that in reality, people who seem weaker are indispensable. They must not be labeled and dismissed."[6] It isn't out of pity or charity that they are indispensable— their very presence is required to allow the gathering of believers to be who God created them to be. They invite believers to better know God and to be in God's presence. Sara Ellet writes of her understanding of Christ and the way it has been impacted by living at L'Arche for all these years.

> I have really lived in viewing Jesus by the smell of Christ. Cooking dinner [with friends with disabilities] smells like Jesus to me. Washing urine out of clothing smells like Jesus to me. Shirts covered in drool smell like Jesus to me. I recognize Jesus and the Holy Spirit by their smell. One can cover up wounds, and wash clothing but you cannot hide the smell of humanity. When a member farts in the van during winter; that is Jesus in the flesh and blood with his dirty, sweaty, farting self right in front of me.[7]

Doing life, being in community with those with disabilities is not a glamorous existence, but it does let us see God. Those with disabilities may seem weak by the standards of the world but they are anything but. They call us all to be more humane, more patient, more reliant on God when we think we can do it on our own strength. The role they play in the body of Christ is vital as we help each other to be more of who God created us to be.

4. Zirshcky, *Beyond the Screen*, 112.

5. McNair, "The Power," 94.

6. Ibid., 97.

7. Sara Ellet, Director of Professional Services for L'Arche Clinton, personal communication, September 29, 2016.

Our perspective changes when we see the role of those with disabilities as vital and not dispensable or a burden. For many, this perspective changes when they themselves have an encounter through a family member, a debilitating accident, or age, that brings disability to the forefront of their existence. In rare instances, churches step up long-term to create space for a once able-bodied member. In most instances, help wanes over time and the now disabled person and their family fade away from regular contact. For too long the church has lived this devaluing attitude.[8] Whether it was intentional or not, the church ignored and isolated those they could not heal, holding up normalization and blending in as the goal rather than owning the diversity created by God. White cites Nancy Eiesland, a theologian with a disability herself, saying "Healing has been the churchly parallel to rehabilitative medicine, in which the goal was normalization of the bodies of people with disabilities."[9] Eiesland goes on to say, "The church is impoverished without our presence. Our narratives and bodies make clear that ordinary lives incorporate contingency and difficulty. We reveal the physical truth of embodiment as a painstaking process of claiming and inhabiting our actually existing bodies."[10] As we encounter and welcome those with bodies different from ours, the body of Christ gets real about the struggles and pains that take place when God's people choose to value all people as equals.

Valuing the role of every member as equal is itself a bold move toward truly being the body of Christ. It is no longer acceptable to be welcoming and allow someone to sit in your space as a permanent visitor who is able to observe but never partake in or give back to the community. For some in our society they experience a cutting off from access to the good things of life many take for granted. These good things include family, friends, a social life, work, good health, belonging, the ability to contribute, and, importantly, faith formation.[11] Wolf Wolfensberger's Social Role Valorization (SRV) is a theory that invites society to choose to value roles others may deem less than productive. McNair offers the following insight from SRV: "Given the prominent values of our contemporary culture, children and

8. George White writes on a wide variety of ways the church devalues those with disabilities drawing from his own experience as well as the writings of several respected contemporary authors in the field of disability and theology. See White, "People with Disabilities in Christian Community," 12–35.

9. Ibid., 12.

10. Ibid., 16.

11. McNair, "What Would Be Better?," 13.

adults with significant physical and/or intellectual impairments tend to be societally devalued, negatively perceived and mistreated, cut off from these good things which we all want."[12] Social Role Valorization seeks to create or support socially valued roles for devalued people in society.[13] If the role of the person is valued, the person has access to the same good things in life a typical person would and the possibility of marginalization and abuse decreases significantly. Alasdair MacIntyre supports this position, saying that it is as much the role of the community surrounding an individual as the impairment that individual has that defines the disability. "What disability amounts to, that is, depends not just on the disabled individual, but on the groups of which that individual is a member."[14] For the church, SRV has the ability to articulate our call to be the body of Christ. It calls us to live what we declare in stating that every part of the body of Christ has value, no part is better than another, and no part is indispensable.

Safeguarding and passing on the traditions

Who we are, in part, is shaped by how we are raised. To this day, in my mind, Christmas dinner means tamales! I can eat them any time of year but they never taste as good and right as they do preparing for Christmas Day. Favorite foods, music, and humor are all things that begin to develop early on and are dependent on what we are exposed to and explore. I've spent a lot of time thinking about this over the years but the stakes have changed now that I am a mother. I am acutely aware that whatever I teach my children in any one given moment will be eclipsed by what they learn from the repeated patterns in our life as a family. Developmental theorists look at this very issue in considering beliefs, attitudes, and values. Typically focused around the passing down of culture from generation to generation, when it comes to faith formation we address these across the lifespan. We as the church carry the task of practicing faith from generation to generation. This includes children, adolescents, and adults. It takes place as we gather regularly. No one time of teaching and no declaration of our beliefs is as influential as the actual regular practice of our rhythms and rituals of

12. Ibid., 13.

13. See www.socialrolevalorization.com for information and resources on the concept of social role valorization.

14. MacIntyre, *Dependent Rational Animals*, 75.

faith. We learn these foundational elements that shape our very being from those with whom we spend time.

Rhythm and ritual is not taught, it is caught. It is what becomes a part of the very fiber of our being from repeated occurrence. Like land that has been shaped by flowing water, and the path of the flowing water shaped by the land around, rhythm and ritual shape our very identity as God's people and the body of Christ. As a camp chaplain this past summer I was able to walk alongside many adolescents in difficult situations. One particular high school girl came to camp just days after her house had burned down and she and her family had to be rescued from it. It also happened to be that she has autism. She had several difficult moments throughout the week for a variety of reasons. Yet, when it came time for evening service, she settled. She was not crying or worried about the fire, what would happen when she went home, or what was going on around her. In fact, she was able to help others know what to do or what was coming as she knew the rhythm and ritual of the evening service so well. I was hanging out with her cabin and asked her once how she knew all of the prayers and what to do and say. She giggled a little and said "I just know it! I do it because I know it and I know because I do it." I wondered as well if she was simply offering rote memory or if there was meaning attached, so I asked. She then went on to explain every element of the service in ways that were simple but not simplistic. She had been shaped and was shaping the other girls in her cabin not by studying and persuading, but by living the very rhythms she had caught over years of being shaped.

One of the gifts and graces offered to us all by many people with a disability is the need for routine. In a world with ever increasing possibilities of input and options, we struggle to escape multitasking and constant change. It is easy to lose focus and get caught up in the next worship service, the next need in the community, the latest trends, and just plain old being so busy that we lose sight of who we are to be as the people of God. People with disability cannot live at this frenetic and fragmented pace. They remind us that we were never intended to be so busy for God that we lost sight of actually being with God. They remind us that when we feel pressured to move and change, lasting change comes from small moves shaping us over time. Whether you are from a liturgical tradition or free church, we all have rhythms and rituals that are being passed down. It is often in these rhythms and rituals that those with disabilities are most clearly able to connect with God and God's people. It is in these same rhythms and rituals that we are all able to most clearly encounter God and God's people. Yet, the very practice those with disabilities encourage, are the very practices they are denied when we do not intentionally include them in church. We are a better church at safeguarding and passing down our beliefs, attitudes, and values when those with disabilities are present.

Our beliefs, attitudes, and values are to be that of Jesus Christ. First Corinthians 15:3 states plainly that Paul is passing on to others what was given to him in the act of Jesus crucified, resurrected, and in particular in concert with Scripture. We are church when we practice and pass down the traditions that shape who we are as a people. There is a reason the phrase *lex orandi, lex credendi* (roughly translated "as we pray, so we believe") has been so significant within the Christian church over the years. It is in the rhythm and rituals of prayer and worship that the paths of faith have been worn smooth for our living. We pass these on so others too may know the path of faith. As people with disabilities are vital in our churches so too are they vital in passing down faith from generation to generation.

A community that creates virtue

Our world is in disarray. It is fragmented and contains only partial understandings of morality. Or so says Alasdair MacIntyre in the opening of his well-known work *After Virtue*.[15] The remainder of the book seeks to understand how we got into this state of disarray and what it might look like for Christians to live virtuously. While there is much that is useful for shaping the conversation in this and many other readings, it is the church which is to create virtue. This may be categorized in two ways: 1) as we serve each other 2) as we serve the greater good. In both we are seeking to live out individually and corporately Micah 6:8 "And what does the Lord require of you but to love mercy, act justly, and walk humbly with your God." This is no mere call to not make waves. On the contrary, it is God requiring that we live in countercultural ways so that others cannot help but notice where worldly systems of power are disrupting the ways of God.

The notion of intentionally including those with disabilities when discussing service to one another is not common. A beautiful exception is that of a caucus statement of the United Methodist Church. Robert Walker writes of this, saying the "theological statement emphasizes trust in God's creation as good, rather than equating disabilities with fear or sin . . . . That stance is

15. MacIntyre, *After Virtue*.

parallel to our view that all members of the church are God's people who work together in ministry."[16] Scripture calls us to come together with all who believe, no exceptions. Acts 2:44–47 tells of those who shared all they had for the greater good. There are no special qualifications for who gets to give and receive, all are expected to participate in reciprocal relationships. The church should be the premier place where those with disabilities are free to be themselves and where others are willing to recognize our need for another and make accommodations. A great embarrassment has been that of the overall response of the church to the passing of the Americans with Disabilities Act (ADA) in 1990. While many churches were already finding ways to be inclusive and make accommodations, there were far too many who pushed back for a variety of reasons. As public spaces were legislating inclusion, our private places of worship retreated in the name of budgets, aesthetics, ignorance, and a variety of other struggles. Nearly thirty years later, many churches are working hard to find ways not only to serve those impacted by disability but to find ways for them to be able to serve. It is a work in process as we move ever closer to being the church God intended.

Just as church should be the one place where those impacted by disability truly are able to find a home, church should also be the place where we are all finding our voice to serve outside our communities. We should be the first in line to advocate for those in need, not reluctantly wondering if it is our place to say anything at all. Marginalization, discrimination, and even violence come in many forms for people with disabilities. It arrives in unwelcomed looks, inappropriate comments, unsolicited touches, taunts, unnecessary questioning, ignoring, and worse . . . much worse. Sullivan and Knutson set the standard for conversations about abuse within populations including disability in 1998.[17] A little over a decade later, they moved their study out of the hospital setting and garnered a sample size of 50,000 participants looking at the prevalence of abuse. What they learned was that the rate of abuse within the population impacted by disability was 31 percent compared with 9 percent in the general population. Both are terrible, but the reality is that simply having a disability makes a person three times more likely to experience violence in the forms of physical, sexual, psychological harm, and neglect. These statistics only begin to tell the story of the discrimination and struggles faced from a society built for typical

16. Walker, ed., *Speaking Out*, 17.

17. Sullivan and Knutson, "The association between child maltreatment and disabilities."

bodies and minds. A key aspect of being church is the signature of being a people who are about unmaking the violence perpetuated in the world and restoring all who have been violated.

It can be difficult to imagine what standing up for those with disabilities might look like. Consider this: few people would say they are comfortable with a teenager with Down syndrome being raped. Even fewer would be motivated to take action toward prevention. Once they know a teenager with Down syndrome, however, hear her story, and embrace her in community, her witness has the potential to change everything. Advocacy for one individual impacts circumstances for all. The advocacy the church is willing to do for one of her own has the power to change the attitudes and values of the community in which it exists. Advocacy can begin before there is a personal connection. It means saying, from the pulpit, in Bible study, in music, in church policy, in the training of the greeters at the doors of the church, that all people are welcome and if something is a barrier, we will work with you to learn how to change. When we live out the truth that each and every person is an equal, the movement is slow and laborious and we become exactly who God desires for us to be.

Community

In many theology books the concept of church and community would be one and the same. They do have a great deal of overlap. Given our modern context, community will be considered separately but as it relates to the church. In fact, when church is as it should be, community is birthed. Community extends beyond a weekly gathering and into the lives and homes of those involved. Community is present for celebrations and sorrow alike. It includes birthdays, weddings, funerals, surgeries, game nights, and cups of tea. Community helps to hold faith when one of its members is too weak in any given moment to do so. Community isn't about skill or performance, it is being together because you are wanted, it is being together because we often are linked in ways unexplainable. Community affirms God's task in the world of reconciling individuals to himself, and others. Stanley Grenz reminds us salvation has always been for the individual and more than the individual simultaneously. Grenz says:

> Classical theology rightly affirms that God's program in the world
> is directed to individuals in the midst of human sin and need . . .
> This emphasis . . . too often settles for a truncated soteriology

resulting in an inadequate ecclesiology. The program of God includes the salvation of the individual, of course, but it overflows the human person in solitary aloneness. Our salvation occurs in relationship, no isolation. Hence God's purpose includes human social interaction.[18]

We were never intended to do this alone!

For many of us, we function in life surrounded by people at work, school, the grocery store, and in our neighborhoods. We get busy and forget the gift of community all around us. For people with disabilities, there are an increasing number of opportunities for community—if you know where to look, have access, and your body is cooperating on a given day. For some people with disabilities, though, their world becomes a parade of professionals who, while being kind, have a job to do and that is the reason they know the person. For the typical world it is easy to take for granted the community built up around us. Dietrich Bonhoeffer's words from a different time and place echo what so many people with disabilities already know. "It is true of course that what is an unspeakable gift of God for the lonely individual is easily disregarded and trodden under foot by those who have the gift every day."[19] This gift of community is just that, a gift. But it is the intended gift of God for all of God's people. We need each other, even when we do not know it. For those who cannot reach out on their own for complications with disabilities, it is incumbent upon the rest of the people of God to notice and reach out lest we are missing a vital part of our community.

From community to friendship

In every community, friendships form. Friendship moves us beyond interactions, common interests, and covenantal gatherings. Friendship is a shared space of intimacy. It's made of the stuff of deep laughter, shared experience, heartache, and being able to just be in one another's presence without a word spoken. Friendship is what we all want, it is to be known. To be known at the deepest levels and in turn to know others. As we form friendships with people with disabilities we all learn what it means to not settle for false replications. For some people with intellectual disabilities, the longing for intimacy is strong but the internal warning systems that they needn't give away

18. Grenz, *Theology for the Community of God*, 626.

19. Bonhoeffer, *Life Together*, 20.

their bodies, their possessions, or their dignity in order to have friendship is not. That is where we as the body of Christ must step into the prophetic task of the church in friendship. When you learn what a true friend is, when you have a friend looking out for you, the abusive substitutes are no longer as easily able to harm the most vulnerable in our society. Friendship, while mutually beneficial, is a bold way to live into the aspect of church mentioned above where we create virtue by preventing harm.

Friendship reflects back to those with disabilities what God has already declared. They are worthy, valued, and most definitely not a mistake. Amos Yong reminds us that friendship is important in our faith development. It makes it "so that the transformative work of the Holy Spirit can shape, usually unobtrusively, those relationships of mutuality for the glory of God. When friendship flourishes—God's friendship with us and God's gift of friendship to us and for us—the us/them or nondisabled/disabled dichotomies are overcome."[20] Friendship then is a spiritual discipline. It is a sacred act to be practiced regularly. It does not happen by accident. In the patristic era of Christianity, the interactions of believers with those with disabilities was often characterized by philanthropy. It was considered to be an act of charity, not one of mutuality.[21] In our current times, far too many of the relationships those with disabilities have are centered around professional services. In what may feel counterintuitive for those who are able bodied or typical in mind, friendship with someone with a disability is anything but charity. In the mystery of friendship, God's people can know and be known in ways that are mutual. Dignity and worth is declared, for those with and without disabilities.

Questions for Reflection and Ministry Application

1. How might a church convey to visitors that those with disabilities are welcome and included?

2. What stumbling blocks to friendship do you experience? What would make a difference to help you truly feel included?

---

20. Yong, *Theology and Down Syndrome*, 187.
21. Caspary, "The Patristic Era," 24–64.

7

HOSPITALITY AND HESED

Isn't welcome enough?

"Hospitality constitutes a better way of framing relations with
strangers than tolerance."—Luke Bretherton

S EVERAL YEARS AGO A friend of mine and his family began attending a
new church. This is never an easy experience for anyone involved but
for this family, it happened to be that my friend, the father, and one of his
daughters were in wheelchairs. The first week was a friendly and gracious
experience with the exception of one major factor; there was no accessible
restroom at the church. The pastor and a few others made an effort to
invite them back and even said they would make changes to accommodate. What was unexpected, is that by the very next week, the bathrooms
had been renovated allowing full accessibility! While not everyone has
the resources to change something physical that quickly, the message was
profound. You are wanted! You are important! And it is more important to
make changes to our space so we can all feel included than to keep things
as they always have been.

Every person has the experience of being an outsider. Those with disabilities have this experience regularly. We've already established that those
with disabilities are indispensable to the church. The church must embrace
the call to fully engage persons with disabilities in community and friendship. Hospitality grounds us further as a theological task and calling. We offer hospitality not out of guilt or a thin veneer of welcome, but because it is
a "quintessential feature of Christianity."[1] Hospitality, like being the people
and body of Christ, requires a reciprocal relationship where no person is
elevated above another. It is more than merely smiling as a greeter at church

1. Beck, *Unclean*, 121.

or offering cookies on a plate for visitors in your home. Hospitality is gritty and messy. It pushes us to live out what we say we believe in unimaginable ways. It demands that we take the full heft of a person and find ways to integrate them meaningfully into the community so that both the person and the community are shaped and reshaped. "There is no other law that appears as frequently as the law in regard to the stranger in the Hebrew Bible . . . . A stranger in Israel was a person without the rights and privileges held by the community. Strangers lived very vulnerable lives and were in constant need of protection."[2]

I've always admired those with the gift of hospitality. I mean those people who, when they host, make everyone who walks through the door feel as if it has been prepared just for them. This can be experienced in a variety of places but is seen most readily in a home. It is no surprise, then, that the biblical root of hospitality is in the home.

Genuine hospitality invites outsiders in, knowing that the guest will change the dynamics of the household itself. Just as Yong stated the Holy Spirit is able to make, largely unobtrusively, mutual changes in friendship, so, too, the Holy Spirit is able to make changes through hospitality for all involved.[3] When a family brings home a baby, adjustments are made to accommodate the new family member, and a new normal is established. We do this almost instinctually when a child is born or adopted. When it comes to church, however, we are fantastic at inviting people in without ever making accommodations or getting to know them beyond a superficial hello.

> In a phrase, God blesses through the stranger. How so? In hospitality the center of gravity lies neither in the home nor in the stranger, neither in host nor guest, but in the God of both who is discovered redemptively in the meeting . . . . As boundaries become fluid, the vulnerable stranger, the one who ostensibly has nothing to offer, becomes a source of enrichment to the reconfigured household. This marks the upbuilding and bonding work of the Spirit, through whom the center of the household—animated by God's economy of grace—is not the inside of a closed circle, protected by fortified walls, but rather on the margins of an open circle. Perhaps, then, in hospitality the Christian community ideally becomes what it is by extending outside if its own identity, by building border crossings that serve as point for reconciliation and partnership instead of

2. Bos, "The Way of Hesed," 13.
3. Yong, *Theology and Down Syndrome*, 187.

separation. This kind of paradox is displayed poignantly in stories of hospitality that depict hosts "entertaining angels unawares."[4]

Hospitality establishes both guest and host as equal and valued. Welcoming someone in is simply not enough. Far too many people who have been marginalized have been invited to the table, only to learn that welcome does not necessarily imply inclusion. In this way, the host maintains a surplus of power over his guest. People with disabilities are often welcomed to sit and watch, welcomed to be present and silent, welcomed to pose for pictures, and welcomed to respond with gratitude for whatever is offered to them. This welcome without inclusion keeps those with disabilities in positions of inequality and subordination. Genuine hospitality rearranges the power dynamic, moving host and guest to equal places with God at the center.

To be the one entertaining presumes you have something to offer. Extending hospitality then is a declaration of the abundance Christ has bestowed. It is giving abundance out of abundance. We hear this in Scripture in 1 John 4:19, "we love because he first loved us." Giving love, entertaining others, is not commanded in order to receive anything in return.[5] Hospitality freely gives out of the overflow of abundance from which we have already received. But what is this abundance and from where does it come? The Bible speaks over and over again of *hesed*. It is a term so thick with meaning that any one translation will offer an anemic rendering.[6] It is the idea of more than enough, plenty, abundance. But it is abundance in love, kindness, righteousness, constancy, devotion, goodness, and more.[7] *Hesed* shouts from the rooftops that we have all we need to be the people of God and live into the theological concept of hospitality. We need not live out of our fear of scarcity.

The Christian world has struggled, knowing it is distasteful to exclude others for their differences including ethnicity, education, morality, sex, and even ability. Instead, we use a "scarcity rationale" to avoid inclusion and integration of those with disabilities. There are three pervasive justifications for excluding people with disabilities that I have heard over the years. The first is that there are no people with disabilities in our church or

4. Reynolds, *Vulnerable Communion*, 243.

5. Jacober and Godfrey, "Hospitality and a God-given identity."

6. *Hesed* may be found in a number of passages but a few are as follows: Exod 34:6–7, Num 14:18, Neh 9:31, Ps 86:15, Ps 145:8, Jon 4:2.

7. Bos, "The Way of Hesed," 10–11.

community. A quick trip to any local school or a look at information from the US Census will dispel that myth.[8] The second justification is that they are afraid they will hurt someone with a disability. I'm going to call that one out. We don't wonder if we are going to harm toddlers, or the elderly. We ask questions on how to best come alongside, we watch, listen, go to trainings, and are willing to come alongside others who know better. We can do the same with people with disabilities. It is wonderful that so many churches are now able to have dedicated leaders and spaces for people with disabilities, but they did not start that way. The third justification has to do with resources. Sometimes it is that there is no trained person, sometimes it is said blatantly that it comes down to money. There is a concern that if changes are made to accommodate someone with a disability, others will leave. Realistically, this will likely be true. Some will leave. But others will come. And those who stay are living into the calling of God and the theological principle of *hesed*. Hospitality is not a zero sum game. There is not "only so much hospitality" to go around. When we include others, we expand our tent not fill it. There are growing pains and all must be willing to relinquish some control. It however not only is possible but preferable according to the mandate of God. Exclusion protects what we believe to be ours; inclusion stewards that which belongs to God. In *hesed* we are taught in word and experience of the unending abundance of God. An abundance of love, or patience, of kindness, and stability. *Hesed* says that there is more than enough to go around and including someone who may need extra time, attention, or money does not mean there will not be enough for others. God promises (1 Kgs 17:12–16) and models (Matt 14:13–21) generosity as a way of having enough. To be hospitable, then, is to follow the teachings of Jesus.

What about the converse? To not extend hospitality speaks to the sin and the woundedness in our world. Too often those with disabilities are not looked at as equals. If we do not consider them equal, then, we rationalize, there is no harm in withholding hospitality. We separate into my tribe and your tribe, into us and them. Beck describes sin as the force that brings about dehumanization and stratification.[9] While our words and even official legislation declare those with disabilities as important, far too many are not experiencing that message. Sin is a power that has such a stronghold that it keeps the justifications happening long after awareness

8. www.census.gov/people/disability.

9. Beck, *Unclean*, 122.

is raised. We, unknowingly, get socialized into patterns of injustice and live contrary to the *hesed* of God. We live contrary when we believe we are not enough, that whatever anxiety or flaw we have will try God beyond any steadfast love that might have been offered. We live contrary when we are concerned with how something might look if we included those who are flawed, forgetting that we are all flawed. We grow accustomed to safety and no longer want to speak out for fear that donors, or parents, or our own family will grow weary of our voice. With each denial of hospitality, we calcify the sin of dehumanization. In a great cosmic irony, there is no limit to how much we can deny Christ and God's provision that *hesed* cannot cover. We only harm ourselves and prevent the work of the Holy Spirit when we deny hospitality. God however has steadfast love and will patiently redeem us from this vicious cycle.

Questions for Reflection and Ministry Application

1. Could someone with a disability get into your home? Church? Place of meeting?

2. Would someone be able to get into your heart? Is your life hospitable? What needs to be rearranged in order for your life to be so?

3. Reflect on a time when you felt unwelcomed. What would it feel like to be unwelcomed by God's people? What conclusion would you make about Jesus as a result? Now reflect on a time when you felt welcomed and answer the same questions.

8

WORSHIP, DISCIPLESHIP, AND VOCATION

How do we participate?

"Children have never been very good at listening to their elders, but they have never failed to imitate them."—James Baldwin

"The place God calls you to is the place where your deep gladness and the world's deep hunger meet."—Frederick Buechner

Worship

FOR PEOPLE WITH DISABILITIES, the daily tasks of life can feel all-consuming. To ask for something more can seem insensitive at best, and cruel at worst. Or is it? Is it possible that asking for daily tasks to be lived in a way that are God honoring is actually a way of honoring others as well? I say yes. Too often those with disabilities have been viewed as projects for ministry, not partners in ministry. We have assumed they will be blessed to be a part of someone else's discipleship even if they do not experience the demands and joys of discipleship themselves. And too often we have assumed that those with disabilities lack the gifts and graces to serve in rich and fulfilling ways. Even those with the most extreme of disabilities are created in the image of God. As such, they have purpose and value in this world. Their value may not be obvious at first. The reality is that they may need extra time and resources but what they bring to the table is worth it. It is in fact priceless.

When I was growing up, the song "I Love You, Lord" was popular at every children's, youth, and adult gathering. Even though I am "vocally challenged," I always liked the song. I particularly liked the line, "May it be a sweet, sweet wound in your ear." I always imagined my off-key, pitch-imperfect singing to be beautiful by the time it reached God. I've always been partial to children's choirs with kids who turn around backwards and some who sing different songs entirely! I've even been known to decide to become a member of a church due to its quirkiness rather than a slick, professionalized presentation. I have volunteered in a number of places where, if you did not come with some serious training under your belt, you were never going to be asked to lead, sing, play, or pray in a corporate setting. Corporate worship always seemed to morph from a time of responding to God to being in awe of the talents of others. I was struck that it left no room for anyone who was less than flawless. Many of my friends with disabilities would not be considered to be a leader in music, liturgy, or even Scripture reading because of the challenges they present. But they are capable of worship. It is the work of the typical community to redefine our approach to worship and recall that perfect is not without flaws. Rather, worship is the posture of being drawn by God into completeness. We may be complete, whole, lacking in nothing as we worship with abandon before God our creator. If you have never been to a gathering of people with disabilities when praise songs and dancing breaks out, I am not certain you have ever seen true worship!

I want to be careful to note that worship is not confined to music or to a corporate setting, but, as this is such a common focus at this point in history, it warrants a small conversation. My husband grew up in the Salvation Army. He has been playing instruments since he was small and music is a part of the very fabric of his being. He often tells me about being in a band where they had to be perfect in the flawless, make-no-mistakes sense so that the band would not be a stumbling block to anyone in worship. There is a discipline, a healthy respect for other worshippers in his approach. Yet this approach can exclude those who cannot perform in certain ways. There is room for an additional perspective.

A few times per semester, one of our students, Donovan, brings his guitar to youth group. He offers a monotone song with the exact same strum pattern throughout, all without changing chords. Even still, not a person is present who is not ushered to the feet of Jesus every time he sings. It is far from flawless, but it is full of leadership and humility. I can't help but wonder if Donovan would have wanted to join the band my husband was in growing up. What might have happened? My hope is that each would grow in their understanding of what it means to worship in song and all would better be led to praise as a result.

Worship, however, is not only about music and corporate gatherings. Worship is where we as Christians begin our daily tasks. It is our response to God's revelation in everything we do. Too many of us, people with disabilities included, have slipped from being active when the notion of perfection loomed large. We moved from the biblical words surrounding *perfect* emphasizing wholeness and the initiative of God to a functional understanding where those in vocational ministry, the professionals, were to handle all matters of corporate worship. Even more, the term *worship* has all but dropped from the discipleship conversation where every believer is invited to respond to God's revelation in every activity of their day. It is difficult to imagine in what way pausing for a nebulizer treatment or needing to talk to others about an aversion to sudden noises could be worship. Our inability to see this connection is more a lack of theological imagination than lack of possibility. My daughter has a friend in her class with has a host of severe allergies. At the tender age of five, Allison had to address this with her entire kindergarten class. Allison's parents sent a letter home to the parents of other children in her class, asking that certain foods not be included in lunches. Quite reasonably, Allison's parents said that, if parents wanted to include some of those foods in their children's lunch, they requested that the child simply eat lunch in the other classroom and rejoin his or her classmates afterwards. One mother refused to comply. She made a very public statement about how this infringed on her rights and that these allergies were all a hoax. Allison's response was astonishing. She was so concerned that the girl whose mother refused to comply would feel isolated, left out, or be teased, that she asked if she, that is Allison herself, could sit at a table alone for every lunch so that she needn't fear an anaphylactic episode and that the other girl could be with her friends. When I asked her why she did that, she simply said because Jesus calls us to be kind even when others aren't. God revealed himself to her and, in what seemed to be a mundane daily task, even a five year old is compelled to respond. That is worship.

Two words in Scripture inform our understanding of worship. The first is *latreia* (Rom 12:1, Matt 4:10, Acts 26:7), meaning worship or service. The second is *leitourgia* (Luke 1:23, 2 Cor 9:12, Phil 2:30), meaning service to the community. Either way, worship is a response to God and that response comes in serving. Serving others as we seek to live that out, we may be entertaining angels unawares. Serving others wondering if he or she is the least of these and actually Jesus in disguise. Serving others through a smile, a prayer, or even being attentive when that is all we have to offer. Worship is service and it is not reserved for the able-bodied and perfect. Worship is what we do, individually and corporately, to experience the ongoing transformation God offers through his perfecting work that makes us whole. It is much easier to hide or use a disability as an excuse not to worship. The onus is on the entire body to create space for someone with a disability not just to be welcomed and sit in proximity to others, but to be fully present and to make an impact on the community by their very presence. When it comes to communal interaction or comprehension of the Christian message, a common question for those in particular with communication struggles or cognitive disabilities is whether they "get it." There is a concern that the message is over the heads or misunderstood. That has much more to do with the comfort of the one asking that question than the reality of the person with the disability. God is mystery and even the most astute and faithful do not fully comprehend everything. In this sense, we are all on a continuum of being able to more or less articulate our understanding of God. As we spend time with other believers, we gain perspective and are able to know more of God. We are called to be fully present with one another as we seek to be fully present with God. In this sense, "the Christian life becomes the communal practice of staying awake in the presence of God."[1] Corporate times exist so that we may grow and remain faithful even in the most challenging of times.

Worship can and should include times of singing, reading Scripture, prayer, proclamation, all the works of the people, and testimony when the body is gathered. These gatherings, however, should be inviting us all to respond in worship to the revelation of God in every area of our lives. With this being the playing field, there is no reason anyone with any level of a disability should not be invited to worship. It is in worship that we both respond to God and grow in our knowing of him. This may be through knowledge or experience, each is equally given by God. For friends with Intellectual and Developmental Disabilities (IDD), it is likely through the experience of the Holy Spirit, liturgy, the rhythm and ritual of time with God that their faith will grow. For others, the cognitive barrier may not be the issue and it is the knowledge of God that draws them into deeper faith. For all of us, it is as we do life together that we spur one another on to love and good deeds.

1. Battles, "How Should We Live?," 288.

Spurring one another on to love and good deeds requires a recipro-cal relationship. Above, I noted that testimony is a vital part of worship. Testimony is the space where we come together to hear from God through one another's voices. Almeda Wright offers a powerful chapter arguing the value and importance of testimony as a hopeful spiritual discipline. The context in which she writes is youth, but the concept cuts across all demo-graphics. She says:

> the practice of testimony empowers youth to "tell it like it is," not to be ashamed of their experiences, but to share their experiences in the hope and knowledge that their stories will be received by an encouraging community, and it will also serve as encouragement for others. The practice of testimony aids in the process of helping youth find their authentic voice, a voice constructed and recon-structed in light of communal witnessing and listening.[2]

What is at the heart of this statement is inclusion. While Wright is addressing the inclusion of youth, it applies no less to those with disabili-ties. The benefits, similarly, apply no less to a person with a disability and to the community of which they are a part. Testimony creates space for authentic storytelling and for the community to affirm and correct those portions that relate to God. Testimony also invites the community to do some self-reflection and consider where their stories warrant affirmation or correction. The cost in testimony is that not everyone will truly listen. To listen requires active presence and the ability to hear someone's story on their own terms. It demands that we not overlay our presuppositions and experiences on someone else. It invites us into the diverse world created by God. This can feel too risky for some. Risky or not, it is what is required. Testimony should give a safe space for those with disabilities to find and practice their voice so they may use it in the world outside of the church. This, too, is a spiritual act of service. This, too, is the act of a disciple.

Discipleship

It is in the life of discipleship that we learn to relate the story of Jesus to our own story. Testimony is a step on the journey of discipleship. To be a dis-ciple, a *mathetai*, was to be more than a student of Jesus. It assumed portions of life being done together, intimacy of personal relations, and a transition

2. Wright, "The Power of Testimonies," 195.

from being a follower to being an adherent. All through the Gospels we read of crowds who gathered around Jesus. The crowds loved to hear his teachings and even followed him at times. It is hard to determine if it was Jesus they were interested in or the relational capital and social scene they were building. When the demands of the actual teaching became more acute, the crowds thinned and disciples remained. These were the people who had been present, worshipped, learned, and sought to align their lives around what Jesus taught. Discipleship is not for the faint of heart. It is, however, the prime place where in our weakness we are made strong. It was through these people that the gospel was spread and world changed.

Those who are a part of a discipleship group or class are often seen as the spiritual all-star team in church settings. Discipleship takes place after the initial conversion but is reserved for those "serious" about their faith. What this often amounts to is extra Bible study and cognitive assent. If your tradition is more charismatic in nature, disciples are the people who pray before and after service, or are gathered for special times of prayer. Disciples are seen as the ones who serve others. As noted above, worship is where service is to take place and worship is open to all. What this has meant in the lives of those with disabilities is that they are often excluded from formal conversations and programs of discipleship. They are not often invited for lectures and discussions, or for special prayer sessions. I want to be clear, being excluded by the program does exclude those with special needs from being disciples. Just because we do not invite them to the program does not mean they are not disciples. What it means is that we as the church are missing out on the work God is doing in and through them. People with disabilities not only have the ability to be loved by Jesus, but to adhere to his teachings and align their very lives around his story.

Discipleship alongside those with disabilities can be a creative, freeing experience. One of my very favorite examples of this comes from a friend who refused to see limitations for the girls in her group. Suzanne Williams is the Regional Young Life Capernaum Director in the Nashville area. In addition to her regular duties leading Club, a youth group experience for people with disabilities, she led a discipleship group. The girls in her group each had their own unique personalities, likes, and dislikes, just like other adolescents. What they each also had was a disability of some sort. Suzanne refused that to be what defined them or their ability to align their lives around God. She invited each girl to choose a project in their discipleship group that had to meet at least one of three categories. It must: 1) glorify

God; 2) grow their faith; or 3) serve others. The young women took this very seriously, studying and talking about what this meant for a year. They prayed for one another as each girl chose a project. This was not a one-off service afternoon. It was an intense time of community where not only the lives of the young women were changed, but so many around them.

The act of discipleship was never intended to take place in isolation. We seem to know that in the church, until it comes to those with disabilities. They are too often seen as a way to connect typical people with serving the least of these. There is a fine line between offering a special program (which we all love) and using those with disabilities as a service project. What if those with disabilities instead were invited into discipleship? Stanley Grenz offers the model of discipleship in which we pattern our lives after that of Jesus and enter into his story.

> The life of discipleship after the paradigmatic life of Jesus takes us out of our separate and separated existence. Jesus becomes the universal human in our experience as we enter the fellowship he offers, the life-in-community to which he directs us. This fellowship is from beginning to end a corporate reality, the community of his disciples.[3]

Instead of excluding or isolating those with disabilities, discipleship invites them into the community and reorients Christ as the center of their lives. This changes the lives of those with disabilities for the better *and* the lives of the other disciples in community who may have otherwise missed out on knowing this other person. This radical inclusion invites all disciples to live the hospitality to which we have been called. It also affirms the doctrine of theological anthropology, naming each person with a disability as worthy and able to participate in the act of intimate relationship with God. This is the heart of discipleship.

Empowerment is the extra benefit that accompanies discipleship. For every person with a disability who has felt devalued, voiceless, isolated, and misunderstood, discipleship is a way to be empowered. It is a way to realize that "our lives make sense as we see that our sinful, alienated past has given way to the present enjoyment of fellowship and the anticipation of the fullness of life-in-community awaiting us in the future."[4] Freedom is a result of this empowerment. In John 8:31–32 (TNIV) Jesus says, "If you hold to my teaching, you really are my disciples. Then you will know the truth, and the

3. Grenz, *Theology for the Community of God*, 382.
4. Ibid.

truth will set you free." Teachings can come in many forms. Teaching can be about knowledge and cognitive assent. Teaching can also be experiential, spiritual, and lived. To pattern our lives after Jesus means that we learn the ways of Jesus not only (or even ever) by sitting in a classroom but by living, sharing testimony, listening, and growing. In the process, freedom from the judgments of this world come. Freedom from feeling less than adequate is replaced with a sense of being God's child, created in his image, and being perfect in the sense of having all you need.

Discipleship calls us to speak out for justice. This can feel scary when it is you who is often the recipient of unjust actions. For those with disabilities, as they find their own voices, the chorus is strengthened. Bonhoeffer warns against a Christianity where idle observation is considered acceptable. "Instead of 'dull looking on', the Christian is called to act as 'vicarious representative' and to open her mouth and hand for the powerless, attacked, despised."[5] Bonhoeffer was acutely aware of the stakes for what he was saying. Nietzsche had launched an attack saying that Christianity's defense of those with disabilities celebrated "suffering and weakness over human strength and excellence."[6] Rather than attack Nietzsche directly, Bonhoeffer took the critique as

> an apologia for the weak: Christianity stands or falls with its revolutionary protest against violence, arbitrariness, and pride of power and with its apologia for the weak. I feel that Christianity is doing rather too little in showing these points than doing too much. Christianity has adjusted itself much too easily to the worship of power. It should give much more offense, more shock to the world, than it is doing.[7]

The writings of Don Kraybill echo this same sentiment, decades later, in *The Upside Down Kingdom*. There, Kraybill writes that "Jesus was an extremist, and we are moderates."[8] We are called to stand up for those without voices. As we learn to communicate, to truly listen, and enter into their stories, we live out a discipleship that cannot help but to speak out for justice. It is a bold move in this world. It is expected from those of us who look to Jesus as our model. It is expected from us as we all—people with disabilities and able bodied—unite in one voice. What I mean by this is that this is not

---

5. Wannenwetsch, "My Strength Is Made Perfect in Weakness," 367.

6. Ibid., 362.

7. Ibid.

8. Kraybill, *The Upside Down Kingdom*, 13.

the role of only those who are able bodied as a sort of caretaking for those with disabilities. Those with disabilities have a role in this advocacy as well. In fact, they just may have the most important role of all. Even still it takes the entire community.

As Christians speak out for those whom society considers to be weak, we can began to make powerful changes, albeit slowly. The value of those with disabilities is affirmed and raised. The understanding that they, too, are true disciples and have something to offer is realized. This realization allows all of us to live into our calling, our vocation.

Vocation

There was a time when those with disabilities would have been considered to be unemployable, unable to contribute to the community in any significant manner. This posture alone denied the possibility of discipleship that leads to vocation for an entire community of people. Thankfully, there are places where this is shifting today. People with disabilities are finding meaningful work as they, too, live out their callings.

It would be prudent to back up and discuss the notion of vocation. In the Old Testament, vocation was a call to a specific person or group of people from God.[9] In the New Testament it was a specific call to follow Jesus or to salvation.[10] Vocation was sacred. It was important and vital in the lives of those in the world God created. It was not necessarily tied to remunerated employment, as so many today would assume. It might well be, and that would be lovely, but that is not what comprises one's vocation. Vocation has a richer theological meaning: vocation is calling. A calling, however, demands an asking of the questions: "By Whom? And For What?"[11] As Christians, as disciples, the answer is clearly a calling by God and for God's purposes, glory, or intent. "Our vocation comes out of our identity, not the reverse."[12] As disciples our identity is in Christ and so the calling of vocation is to do whatever you do as if working for the Lord and not humankind. Working for the Lord can have the dangerous possibility of being seriously misunderstood. It can shackle a person to a works-based theology of trying to earn the love of God. It can be clouded

9. Atkinson, "Vocation," 711.

10. Ibid.

11. Stevens, "Vocational Guidance," 1079.

12. Ibid., 1080.

by a culture that values doing over being. Many Christians and even ministers spend so much time running from ministry to ministry, writing, speaking, organizing, *doing* in the name of Jesus, that they live into the anxiety of the world rather than the abundance of God. That doesn't have to be the end of the story. Vocation does not mean being overwhelmed and overworked in the name of Jesus. Living into our vocation can free us into a God-given way of being.

Vocation invites everyone to this way of being. Vocation is birthed from our worship and discipleship as we spend time with God. It was God who set the rhythm and ritual of life to spend time regularly together, to Sabbath. It is in Sabbath where we rest, create, and recreate or play. It is a compelling not just to be about the business of God or doing things for God, but to actually be present *with* God. Jaco Hamman talks of this time with God as play. This is not mere frivolous play. In fact, there is no frivolous play! It is play where we are freed from the constraints of a world demanding flawless production and into a world of complete purpose. This can feel too difficult if not impossible in a world imposing interpretations of differences as limits. Limits, however,

> are inherent to life, yet one can experience life as flowing, abundant, inexhaustible, endless, unfailing, infinite, ceaseless, and everlasting despite those limits. Play-fullness is boundless and beckons you to move beyond a life constrained by boundaries and limits .... *A life the reverberates with vitality and energy is possible.* This life may remain elusive if life-giving and life-affirming energy rarely flows, first to you and them from you to enrich and nurture others. Boundlessness invites you to discover something new about yourself, others, God, nature, and life in general.[13]

Play ties into vocation as it frees us to answer a question posed by Hamman, "How do you flow, in life-affirming ways, to others or to your community?"[14] Vocation then is your play-full act of discipleship. It is what brings life to you and those around you in ways that honor God. It may look like speaking up for yourself or others in need, it may look like delivering homemade cookies, or offering a kind word when you see others. It may take place in very public arenas of service, or in the privacy of your own space offering prayers for those in desperate need. It is necessary for the

13. Hamman, *A Play-Full Life*, 76.
14. Ibid.

spiritual and emotional health of every Christian, and is the right of every person with and without a disability.

I've already established that those with disabilities have every possibility of being a disciple of Jesus. Consequently, they, too, have done all that is required for meaningful vocation. For too many centuries we simply did not acknowledge the gifts and graces those with disabilities brought to the church, and the world and church were the worse for it. As an awakening has been taking place, we can no longer rest in the act of service to those with disabilities, but must live into service with them.

To live in service with others demands that we value one another completely. Ephesians 5:1 lays out a picture of what it looks like to serve in unity within the context of a vocational call. It says, "I, therefore, the prisoner in the Lord, beg you to lead a life worthy of the calling to which you have been called, with all humility and gentleness, with patience, bearing one another in love, making every effort to maintain the unity of the bond of the Spirit in the bond of peace" (NRSV). We are called not only to vocation, we are called to vocation with one another. It behooves us as followers of Christ not only to serve out of the integrity of our own discipleship, but to create ways and include others to do the same. Those with disabilities may not have the same gifts and graces as typical people, but then again, they may! Regardless, they do have gifts and graces. In the New Testament our calling to salvation is not only one of being saved from something, but being saved for something. That something for which we are saved is our vocation. When we really lean into discipleship, vocation is the natural result.

Questions for Reflection and Ministry Application

1. At which level of involvement with brothers and sisters with disabilities is your church or ministry?

    a. we have never thought about people with disabilities being part of our community

    b. we put on some sort of yearly event with people with disabilities

    c. one or more persons with a disability is present in our community

    d. they are included in the various opportunities for fellowship with us

    e. we have studied and removed all obstacles of accessibility physical and relational within our community

    f. they are a vital part of our community serving and using their gifts in a variety of settings including forms of leadership

2. Whichever level you are at, what steps could you as a community take to get to the next level over the course of the next year?

3. If you are part of a small group would your group consider inviting someone with a disability as a member? Why or why not?

4. What attitudes or misplaced beliefs caught your attention in this chapter regarding a full inclusion of those with disabilities in worship, discipleship and vocation?

9

SCRIPTURE

How is disability addressed in the Bible?

> "Do not try to make the Bible relevant. Its relevance is axiomatic.
> Do not defend God's word, but testify to it. Trust to the Word. It is
> a ship loaded to the very limits of its capacity."
> —Dietrich Bonhoeffer

How can I understand God, through the Bible, given the reality of disability?

For the past several years I have had the privilege of getting to view the world through the eyes of children. I have three little ones at home and they are never short on opinions or things they want to share with me. This also means that I am particularly well versed in kid culture at the moment. Playlists and personalizable technology dominates the adult world. For children, there is a similar approach for kids to find a toy that is designed just for them. American Girl has done a particularly good job of this creating a series of "Just Like Me" dolls, complete with the ability to choose skin color, freckles or no freckles, eye color, and hair color and style. Recently they added a series not as special stock or a novelty item but just as part of their regular line where you can design a doll with no hair, or with cochlear implants, a wheelchair, braces, and even a diabetic kit to be worn around the doll's waist. While still not fully represented, children are growing up in a world where disability is the most integrated it has ever been. And yet, many people with disabilities still do not see many models of someone just like them included in leadership, in church life, or even in Scripture. The passages of Scripture where disability is mentioned have far too often been preached or taught as a spiritual disability, not a physical or mental one.

A closer reading of the Bible allows us to see with new eyes a much wider array of people included in Scripture.

Early on in my teaching career I had to face my own rhetoric. I was teaching a course called "Orientation to Theological Studies" at Fuller Seminary while working on my PhD. The very first semester I taught that course, a blind student, whom I'll call Henry, enrolled. Fortunately, Fuller's office of accommodation was on it and the syllabus had already been put into braille. Henry shared that he had been blind since birth. I realized how much of his life he spends educating and inviting others into his world. He told me he would often sit with his eyes closed to listen to class lecture and conversation but that he was not sleeping. He asked if I could spend a few extra moments with classmates introducing themselves and if they would say their names when speaking so he could get to know each one. We talked of ministry, school, and faith. And one day, we talked about Scripture. Henry had a love for Scripture and knew the well-worn pages of his Bible. He also had a deep desire that those in class realized that the Bible named people just like him. Some had been blind since birth and were healed (John 9:1–12), others were blind and not healed (Luke 14:7–15). That one conversation in that one class has played over and over as I talk with people with disabilities looking for passages where they can find themselves. They are aware that Scripture is for everyone and that most of it fits us all but it has been taught that their particularities do not matter and any mention of a disability was only a metaphor for something else. They were taught that the Bible has little to nothing to say to them about God when it comes to disability. Henry made it clear, those passages were not metaphors. He is not a metaphor. His blindness is real. And the Bible has something to say to him and others with disabilities.

The Bible does have a lot to say as a specific revelation of God. Before naming several passages, a more general look at Scripture will be helpful. There are many ways to talk about Scripture, including who wrote it, how we got it, and ways to study it. Those are conversations for another time and place. For this writing, the concern comes from the question, How can I understand God, through the Bible, given the reality of disability? The Bible is God's most clear, tangible revelation we hold in common with the church visible and invisible. Many theologians explain Scripture as God's self-disclosure of who God is and who God wants people to be. This means we get to know God, in part, through Scripture. Here I will borrow from Migliore and use his analogy of knowing God interpersonally through scripture.[1] With this analogy "we assume that persons are embodied agents who disclose their identity and intentions in their words and actions, an analogy between knowledge of other persons and the personal self-disclosure of God to us can be developed."[2] According to Migliore, knowledge of persons requires four things: "attention to persistent patterns," the ability to be "free to do new and surprising things," "a continuous invitation to trust and live in response to promises," and our identity is "rendered in narrative forms."[3] Each one of these elements helps to better understand the arc of scripture as well as the revelation of God.

It is important to pause for a moment to talk of the arc of scripture. The order of the Bible was set during canonization and considered settled by the fifth century CE. The order of Scripture however has not always been set. In fact, the Old Testament or Hebrew Bible is shared by Jewish and Christian traditions but holds a vastly different order. Within the Jewish community, the order was set, more or less, according to the time period in which the books were written. It began with Torah or teachings, added the Nevi'im or prophets, and closed with Ketuvim or writings. This would have been the order during the time of Jesus whether he used the Hebrew Bible or the Septuagint. As the Christian church was established, faithful followers of God were trying to make sense of Jesus and how this all fit together. The order established in the Christian Old Testament uses the exact same books but a different order, emphasizing the story of God preparing his people for the Messiah. So, the Christian order of the texts ends with Malachi proclaiming, "Behold, I am going to send you Elijah the prophet before the coming of the great and terrible day of the Lord. He will restore the hearts of the fathers to their children, and the hearts of the children to their fathers, so that I will not come and smite the land with a curse" (Mal 4:5–6). For the Christian Old Testament, the order in which the events took place takes precedence over the order in which the books were broadly written. Why this really matters is that it is important to note that when talking of the arc of Scripture, there is a distinction between the chronology of when it was written and the story that is being told. Clearly the Old Testament is written before the New Testament but exact dates for older works are debated. What is important is the purpose of these texts. The

1. Migliore, *Faith Seeking Understanding*, 36.

2. Ibid.

3. Ibid., 36–37.

Bible is about God. That would seem rather obvious, but it has been used in so many different ways that this simple truth can get lost. It was written by real people, in real contexts, and influenced by the world around them. As modern readers, we must keep in mind that they were doing the best they could with the knowledge and experience they had. The entire arc of Scripture is, and always has been, pushing toward inclusion of those people deemed as other. The text starts out with the Israelites as God's chosen people. By the time Isaiah is prophesying, a small host of ethnicities and people are faithful to Yahweh. By the time of Jesus and beyond, we hold fast to the revelation that following Christ is for everyone, everywhere. We see this arc within the realm of disability beginning in Leviticus 21:16–23 where those with disabilities are not qualified for the priesthood. And yet, Moses, who stuttered, was the leader of the Exodus. By the time we get to Jesus, the poor, the crippled, the blind, and the lame are being called out because they are wanted by God! The arc of Scripture is clear: those with disabilities have always been present and are equal with all others before God. God knew this; it was his people who had to catch up.

Let us return to Migliore's four approaches to knowing God within Scripture. The first approach is looking at the persistent patterns within the texts. God's persistent pattern includes those with disabilities. Arguably the earliest mention of a disability in Scripture is that of Moses in Exodus 4:10–12. Moses protests that he cannot do what God is asking and God's response isn't one of encouragement or comfort. God simply states that whether one is slow of speech, deaf, or blind, all are made by God. God goes further, telling Moses he is qualified to lead. When Moses protests, Scripture says God gets angry (Exod 4:14). This may seem really harsh but what it means is that God viewed Moses, a man with a disability, as capable and not needing to be treated gingerly. Even in God's anger, God provides an accommodation. Moses is still the leader. Aaron, Moses's able-bodied brother, is his mouthpiece. Even in the troublesome passage in Leviticus, a wide variety of disabilities are listed meaning that people with those conditions were in and among their community. They were not isolated, cast away, or worse, left to die on their own. Their very existence was not even questioned. People with disabilities were a fact of life.[4]

---

4. It is important to note here that the ancient Israelite mind-set would not have asked the same questions our modern minds ask. The Israelites pondered God, who God was, and how to best serve and worship God. Our modern minds ask who we are to God and what it means to be human. That would never have occurred to them.

There is a persistent pattern of disability used as a metaphor. Throughout Scripture we see blindness, deafness, and being mute or silence as a metaphor (Ps 115:4–7, Jer 6:10, Isa 42:19–20, Mic 7:16). While this often is used in ways to describe that which is undesirable, it is a reflection on the community choosing disability or acting in ways that are disabled when that is not what God intended or created them to be. In Isaiah 56:10 we read, "Israel's sentinels are blind, they are all without knowledge; they are all silent dogs that cannot bark; dreaming, lying down, loving to slumber" (NRSV). Isaiah 35:5–6 speaks of the restoration God promises to Zion: "Then the eyes of the blind shall be opened, and the ears of the deaf unstopped; then the lame shall leap like a deer, and the tongue of the speechless sing for joy. For waters shall break forth in the wilderness and streams in the desert." These metaphors were much more commentary on people being other than God created them to be than on the acceptability or not of disability. Taking a cue from the Isaiah passage, what follows is the beginnings of having our eyes opened and our ears unstopped regarding the presence of disability in scripture. It is far from an exhaustive list, but it does show a clear presence and inclusion for those with disabilities throughout Scripture.

The following discussion is arranged by broad descriptions of disability, listing several passages and salient points we can take from them. For some, disability is present from birth. For others it is acquired through accident or illness. For nearly all of us who live into old age, one or more disabilities that alter our way of life will be acquired. Beyond these, some disabilities are visible and others invisible. As with many modern concepts, there was no understanding or even category for mental illness during biblical times, yet even glimpses of this may be seen throughout Scripture. It is important to note that disability does not only impact the individual with the disability. There is a great impact on the family, friends, and society in which he or she exists. The Bible speaks even to this.

From Birth

Some disabilities are present from the very first day someone is born. John directly addresses this in chapter 9 of his gospel. The scene opens as Jesus sees a man blind from birth. This, then, prompts the question of why. Is it his own fault? Is his blindness due to his parents? Who sinned? Today, we have a great deal of information regarding the physical conditions of children that occur at or before birth. This is amazing. We know so much more now than they did in biblical times. It is bound to affect our understanding of theology. Some conditions are due to the effects of genetics (Trisomy 21), and others are due to the effects of environment (Fetal Alcohol Syndrome). Both have physical and cognitive manifestations in the lives of individuals. In any case, while we understand these conditions better now, in biblical times they were still struggling to understand why they were experienced.

Blindness, in particular, was commonly tied to struggle. As we see in John 9, there was a notion that sin could cause blindness. It was viewed as an accursed position in life creating many hardships and eliminating opportunities. People born blind were ineligible for priesthood (Lev 21:18) and frequently had to turn to begging (Mark 10:46). Even still, early on there were protections set in place for people who were blind. The law prohibited misleading anyone who was blind (Deut 27:18) or doing anything that would cause someone who is blind to stumble (Lev 19:14). What this means is that there were those with blindness in their midst. Other disabilities present within the community also fall into these same categories or exclusion, but it is blindness that is named distinctly from birth. It is understandable that Jesus is confronted with the question of who sinned causing this disability. Nearly every parent or adult with a disability alive has entertained this very question at some point in his or her life. Many people with disabilities have been plagued by the misperception that sin is intrinsically linked to their very existence. Jesus is asked "who sinned?" as an indictment on blindness. Jesus makes it plain that this is the wrong question. Neither the man nor the man's parents sinned causing his disability since birth. Blindness is a fact of life for some, not something for which we need to assign blame. The onus is on all of us to find a different approach to his disability.

From Injury

Accidents can also cause disabilities. Car accidents, sports, and simple playground activities can contribute to the number of persons with disabilities we have among us. There are also circumstances that increase the risk of accident such as those whose age or health events, like a stroke, can make what would otherwise be an annoying fall turn into a broken hip or other debilitating condition. Abuse and violence are also counted among the culprits of causes of disability. Even with the possibilities being seemingly endless, only about 10 percent of those who have acquired a disability in their lifetime have done so from an accident, as opposed to illness.[5] While 10 percent may not seem like a lot, to the hundreds of thousands of people impacted by the onset of disability, it is significant.

The Bible is not silent on the issue of disability due to injury and accidents. Jacob wrestles with God (Gen 32:24–31). After a night of wrestling, the socket of his thigh is dislocated and Jacob is left with a limp. A strong man, a patriarch of our faith, walked with a limp for the remainder of his days. Perhaps more notable is the story of Mephibosheth. He was not born with a disability. Rather the son of Jonathan acquired it when, at the age of five, his nurse sought to flee to safety with him and dropped him. From that point forward, he was lame (2 Sam 4:4). He returns as a person in the life of David as David is elevated to King over Israel and Judah. David is often credited with kindness to Mephibosheth, seeking to be kind to someone from the house of Saul for the sake of Jonathan. David is reminded of Mephibosheth and his condition. Mephibosheth is crippled in both feet (2 Sam 9:3). Again, in verse 13 it is mentioned that Mephibosheth is lame in both feet. His disability is tied to nearly every mention of him. This is clearly significant for the authors of this text. One way to read this is certainly to honor David for including someone who has such a significant disability. Another plausible reading is to note that it would have been common practice at the time for a king to keep any possible enemies close at hand. Mephibosheth was the son of Jonathan and could easily lay claim to the throne. It may be that despite Mephibosheth's disability, or perhaps because of it, that he was a man of strong character and connection. David knew the potential danger and needed the constant reminder that disability or no, Mephibosheth was not to be trifled with. These two men (Jacob and Mephibosheth) with significant stories in Scripture were distinctly disabled through accident and injury, but they are not the only ones. We addressed this more fully in the section on Jesus, but it is important to recognize that he, too, suffered injury on the cross, having been broken to the point of death. In no more powerful place than in his suffering and death on the cross may we see the presence and strength of possibility for disability.[6]

5. http://www.disabilitycanhappen.org/chances_disability/disability_stats.asp, updated July 2013, accessed September 2016.

6. For more on this discussion see Eiesland, *The Disabled God*.

From Illness

Roughly one in four of today's twenty-year-olds will have a disability before they retire.[7] While it can be difficult to determine exact numbers, one way to estimate the number of those with disabilities is through the office of Social Security and those claiming disability benefits. A little over 8 million or roughly 5 percent of the wage-earning population was receiving disability benefits in 2012.[8] These numbers do not appear to be decreasing any time soon. They are, in fact, on the rise. Of those with acquired disabilities, 90 percent acquire a disability as a result of illness.[9] The very icon for disability, a person on a wheelchair against a blue background, is pervasive at this point. It was not intended only to signify accessibility for those in a wheelchairs, but remains the easiest graphic across cultures to communicate accessibility in public space. Realistically, not everyone who acquires a disability will end up in a wheelchair. Not everyone who acquires a disability will have an obvious external sign that can be noted in a passing glance or even on first meeting. And still, millions will be living with a disability acquired through a life-altering illness. Disability is more common than most of us think. As the church, it is time we were proactive in our thinking and action regarding those with disabilities.

My deep introduction to the world of disability came while I was a PhD candidate, living with a vibrant, fiery woman named Carolyn Vash. She and her husband were in the habit of taking on a student to be her personal assistant in exchange for housing. She herself was a PhD, a professor, a psychologist, and a disability activist. She was also a quadriplegic. Her disability was acquired as a teenager after a bout with polio. She lived this reality when far too many others like her were being hidden away in homes and denied access to basic dignities of life. She simply refused that model and fought for others. She was more than willing to find ways to take care of herself and take care of others. Her life was marked by a disease that left her untouchable for a season, and changed the course of her actions for the good of others.

Second Kings tells a similar story of four lepers living at the entrance of the gate to Samaria (7:3–20). The disabling disease they had would have

---

7. U.S. Social Security Administration, Fact Sheet February 7, 2013.

8. U.S. Social Security Administration, Disabled Worker Beneficiary Data, December 2012.

9. U.S. Social Security Administration, Disabled Worker Beneficiary Data, December 2012.

also rendered them unclean in that society. The situation in the city had become dire due to the siege by an invading army. Death seemed certain. The four leprous men weighed their options, knowing staying at the gate would result in starvation, entering the city would result in starvation, and approaching the camp of their oppressors, the Arameans, could result in sudden death. Knowing that two options offered certain death and the other option offered only the risk of death, the lepers chose to enter the camp of the Arameans. Much to their surprise, it was deserted yet supplies remained, including the most important supply: food. They ate, drank, and then decided to share what they had. Despite being isolated themselves, they realized that they, even they with a disability, had something to offer to others in desperate need.

From Age

Very few of us who live well into old age will avoid disability of some type. As age settled in, many saints found in the Bible needed assistance (Isaac in Gen 27:1, Jacob in Gen 48:10, Elijah in 1 Sam 4:15, and Ahijah in 1 Kgs 14:4). Psalm 71:9 offers the poignant cry that could be echoed today, "do not cast me off in the time of old age; do not forsake me when strength fails." These verses refer to diminished sight and strength, and the reduced capacity for the Activities of Daily Living, commonly known as ADLs (eating, bathing, dressing, toileting, transferring [walking], and continence). Age changes our independence. Even for the greatest of leaders and strongest of people, age ushers in the possibility of disability for the waning years of life. God however is still present and values those with who have been rendered disabled through age.

From Mental Illness

There are times when we all feel that God is distant or unreachable. For some, this sense of abandonment gives way to a perpetual sense of depression and anxiety. Severe depression can be debilitating and interrupt daily life. In biblical times there were no categories for mental illness. In fact, the common thought was that those who processed differently or struggled with clear thinking, voices, or anxiety were likely possessed. Even today a quick Google search regarding mental illness and faith or Scripture will lead to a host of writings offering a cure by leaning into God through prayer and Scripture readings. The unwritten message is that if this does not work, there is something wrong with your faith. There are increasingly writings that encourage a hybrid of leaning into God and the wisdom God has given to doctors and therapists to cope with a wide variety of mental illnesses. Still, the stigma is real and many who suffer do so in silence and isolation.

It is clear in several places in Scripture that mental illness was present. While no one diagnosis is named, the general feeling of abandonment, depression, anxiety, overwhelming life circumstances, and hopelessness are present. These may be read in a variety of places including Job 7, Psalms 13, 22, 42, and Jeremiah 20. In each passage there is a sense of the absence of God and internal anguish making it difficult if not impossible to continue in everyday activities. Jeremiah offers a series of confessions where the progression of his depression becomes clear. These confessions are not of sin, rather, they are complaints against God. "There are seven such confessions (11:18–23; 12:1–6; 15:10–21; 17:14–18; 18:18–23; 20:7–13; 20:14–18) in which the prophet describes feeling abandoned by God."[10] This gives way to Jeremiah being consumed with his own struggles and declaring as cursed the day he was born. Abandoned, isolated, paranoid, confused, weary, feeling out of control, having spare moments of clarity, all of this and more is the reality Jeremiah presents. This internal angst resonates with those who struggle with mental illness today.

Job 7:15–16 speaks plainly of the depths to which depression can take some people, even if only temporarily. Job says that his very soul is suffocating and that his desire would be for his body to join in this suffocation to the point of death. This is mid-story and despite being the long-suffering servant many of us were taught about in Sunday school, Job is struggling, deeply. This is also a far cry from the Job we read in chapter 1:21 with the common refrain that "God gives and God takes away, blessed be the name of the Lord." This notion of God being the one to give *and* take away has become so pervasive that it is difficult to undo but undone it must be. This is what Job says immediately after the crisis of losing his children. He must have been in shock and leaning into what he had always known. By chapter seven of Job's story, the struggle does not let up and Job is being changed by it. By the end of Job the correction to his statement in chapter 1 verse 21 arrives. It is God who restores that which Satan had taken away. God does not toy nor play with us, even in depression or mental illness. It is God who is present and seeking to restore each individual and

10. Knight and Levine, *The Meaning of the Bible*, 441.

the community surrounding. Even as they gave bad advice Job's friends wanted what was best for him. God then comes along through Job's family and directly to restore Job after his suffering. God works through a variety of people for those in need.

From Intellectual and Developmental Disabilities (IDD)

The popular conversation about the rise in behavioral, intellectual, and developmental disorders can hardly be overstated. It increasingly has become the talk of parents, schools, the medical field, and even churches for the past decade. This is all likely for good reason as reported in the March 11, 2016 Morbidity and Mortality Report of the Center for Disease Control (CDC). In this report, the CDC finds that more than one in seven American children between the ages of two and eight have a behavioral, developmental, or intellectual disability.[11] The discussion surrounds the concern that while these IDDs are identified in childhood, they persist well into adulthood and impact education, healthcare, employment, and housing. While the heightened awareness is new, its existence is not.

For many of us who regularly work with those with an IDD, it is common to note that our friends often tap into spiritual truths far more easily and at a greater depth than many of us who are typical. Paul writes to the church at Corinth, calling them, and consequently all of us, to consider this upside-down kingdom. In this passage those who may be considered foolish and despised are actually closer to God in wisdom and nobility (1 Cor 1:25–29). In Paul's rebuke, we find also his encouragement. Amos Yong says of this passage, "if people with intellectual disabilities represent the foolishness of the world, what hinders our viewing them as embodying the wisdom of God?"[12] Yong speaks from experience, having spent his adult life pondering this very idea after formative years growing up with a brother who has Down syndrome. As we read Scripture more carefully and include those whom the world excludes, we will all benefit from wisdom that defies the logic of this world.

11. http://www.cdc.gov/mmwr/volumes/65/wr/mm6509a1.htm?s_cid=mm6509a1_w.
12. Yong, *The Bible, Disability, and the Church*, 98.

For Friends of Those with Disabilities

Mark 2:1–12 and Luke 5:17–26 tell the story of the paralytic lowered through the roof for healing. While it is the paralytic who is healed, the story is about his friends as much as it is about him. Luke 5:20 makes this clear when it is the faith of the friends, not the paralytic himself, that brings about the forgiveness of sins. The pushback from the Pharisees is what pushes Jesus to extend cure, and not just healing. The paralytic himself, while the beneficiary of the entire incident, is merely present. We have no backstory into the lives of the friends or how the man became paralyzed. What is known is that there was a distinct friendship, time spent together, so much so that these friends were willing to do whatever it took to get their paralyzed friend in front of Jesus. They physically carried him to the home, physically carried him up to the roof, dug through the roof themselves, and lowered him down. They were willing to go the distance, to be inconvenienced, because their friend was worth it. Not all relationships are easy or convenient. Not all friendships appear mutually beneficial but there is much to be reciprocated when true friendships form between those with disabilities and those who are typical. Both are blessed. Both are invited into deeper faith as God is at work in all our lives.

For Those Who Don't Know How to Interact with Those with Disabilities

It is so easy to assume that those with disabilities have everything they need. In particular it is easy if we don't even cross paths with anyone with a disability. When we do, the first words out of their mouths are rarely "help me." Jesus, however, always sees those with disabilities and knows them. He knows their condition and the struggles they face. Importantly, he still extends dignity by addressing them directly. In John 5:1–9, Jesus meets just such a man at the pool of Bethesda. This man is lying in wait for the pools to be stirred and Jesus notices him. He knows he has been there waiting for thirty-eight years. For thirty-eight years others have passed by him while helping others. For thirty-eight years, no one offered to carry this man to the pools for healing. The passage does not mention if the man ever asked for help. He may have asked many times only to unheard or ignored. This time, however, Jesus asks him, "Do you wish to get well?" (5:6). It's a simple question, yet one that is layered with compassion and dignity. Jesus doesn't just heal him without asking what he might actually want. Jesus doesn't talk around him but addresses the man directly. Jesus doesn't scold him for not finding the right helper, or agency, or for not speaking boldly enough on his own account. Jesus heals him. Plain and simple, Jesus asks the sick man lying by the pool what he wants and then makes it happen, no more, no less.

From Exclusion to Leadership

Any discussion of Scripture and disability would be incomplete if it avoids the difficult passages. Few passages are more difficult than Leviticus 21:16–24. It is here that Moses is commanded by God to tell Aaron that any descendent of his with a defect of any kind is excluded from the priesthood. And the list of defects is long. It includes being blind, lame, disfigured, having a deformed limb, broken foot, broken hand, hunchback, eczema, dwarfism, a defect in your eye, crushed testicles, or even scabs. While there is much to say about this list and the prohibition for leadership, let's take a glass-half-full approach. This list presupposes the presence of those with disabilities in the community! While excluded from leadership, it is clearly stated that they are to be present and included in the eating of bread from the most holy of sanctuaries. Those with disabilities are spoken of not as a matter of "if" they should be included, but when they are included. They are present. They are not an exception, nor an anomaly. They were prominent enough to warrant an actual conversation. While it may seem appalling to exclude those with disabilities from leadership, it is more appalling to think of our recent history in the church where those with disabilities are frequently absent.

While this Levitical prohibition existed, there were other examples of candidates who were "less than ideal" for ministry. Burd and Barta note several candidates in their writing on the intersection of disability and God's calling to ministry. They "include Moses (Exodus 3 & 4); Aaron and some of his sons (Exodus 28, 32; Leviticus 8, 10); Jonah (Jonah 1–3:10); eleven of the original twelve disciples (Matthew 4:18–22; Mark 1:16–20; Luke 5:1–11; John 1:35–42); and the apostle Paul (Acts 9:1–31)."[13] Paul is perhaps the best known to rise to leadership out of a disability and later confess to an ongoing issue. We read in Acts of his blindness that preceded his conversion. Remarkable as this is, it is his statement in 2 Corinthians 12:7 that testifies to the coexistence of being a leader and the presence of

13. Burd and Barta, "No Limits," 76.

a physical struggle. There has been much speculation over the centuries as to what, exactly, Paul's thorn in the flesh was. What can be known is that it was something that was chronic and unwanted. He names it as a weakness and places it in relation to insults, distresses, persecutions, and difficulties. Whatever this thorn was, it would certainly have taken him out of leadership by the Levitical standards. Yet, we know God used him mightily in his own time and for centuries beyond.

Disability is a fact of life. It was a fact of life in biblical times. Throughout the scriptures we read of a wide variety of people, including those with disabilities. We have been so conditioned to spiritualize every passage we read that we may have missed the direct messages present all along. Even for those who have been advocates, it can feel like pushing a boulder uphill to get others to actually read the passages for what they are. Even this physical weariness is nothing new. Our sentiments echo Paul in 2 Corinthians 4:16: "Therefore do not lose heart. Though outwardly we are wasting away, yet inwardly we are being renewed day by day" (TNIV). We can be renewed by reading Scripture. It provides for us, whether typically or differently abled, a precedent of actual, real disability being engaged in the life of a faith community.

Questions for Reflection and Ministerial Application

1. Talk with a Christian who has a disability to ascertain how they see themselves in Scripture.

2. Read Scripture with a new lens by reading references to disability in a literal sense. How does your perception change?

10

SUFFERING AND HOPE

Is God with me?

> "Hope is willing to leave unanswered questions unanswered and unknown futures unknown. Hope makes you see God's guiding hand not only in the gentle and pleasant moments but also in the shadows of disappointment and darkness."—Henri Nouwen

N O ONE NEEDS TO be convinced of the existence of suffering. Even small children understand that pain happens or that sometimes people are unkind to one another. But what about those people who live in the liminal space between hope and suffering on a daily basis? Concentration can be difficult due to the pain in their bodies, the knowledge that others are making fun of or abusing them. For the young adult who knows they have a disability, marriage is less likely than for the typically abled. That knowledge is painful. There is a different kind of suffering for the loved ones of those with disabilities. Parents who buy nebulizers so their child can breathe easier search for cute masks to make wearing the nebulizer more tolerable. Parents who know how amazing their own child is despite the years and tears to get it has taken to understand him wonder if anyone else will ever have that kind of patience and investment. We could certainly look to world history to note the suffering of those with disabilities in numerous horrors over the centuries. For all of this, the presence of suffering is more real and tangible in our Christian lives than any discussion of suffering. Our theology of suffering is under-examined. Borrowing from Loder, suffering is the "sense of nothingness and abandonment, the cosmic loneliness for all that the primal experience of [God] connoted."[1] In suffering lies lack of "control, bad

---

1. Loder, *The Logic of the Spirit*, 241.

conscience and fear of social exclusion and inferiority."[2] This describes the daily experiences for too many people with disabilities. They lack control of their body or mind. There can be a deep sense of exclusion. Suffering is what we have in the experiential atrocities of life. Suffering is also known by God. As God hangs on the cross we learn, "God knows what suffering is and that it is an inescapable part of the creation."[3] In an ironic twist, it is often creation that imposes the social conditions that bring about suffering.

Suffering is often explained as that mysterious struggle that is either brought about or allowed so that God's glory may be realized. Indeed, it is true that God can be glorified in the midst or the aftermath of suffering. A common argument states that the purpose of suffering is to glorify God. Paul writes, "I consider that our present sufferings are not worth comparing with the glory that will be revealed in us" (Romans 8:18 NIV). And, "for our light and momentary troubles are achieving for us an eternal glory that far outweighs them all" (2 Corinthians 4:17 NIV). The problem with the interpretation of suffering being for the revelation of God's glory is that it is not in the text. That glory will be revealed and that glory will overshadow all suffering is true, but that does not necessitate that God needed suffering for glory to exist. That argument is simply not consistent with the attributes of God discussed earlier in this book. We know this: suffering exists in this broken, fragmented, sinful world. We also know that God is ever working in and through our suffering to redeem that which was meant for evil. This we know from the Psalmist, "the righteous person may have troubles, but the Lord delivers him from them all" (Psalm 34:9 NIV). Psalm 30:5 says, "Weeping may last for the night, but a shout of joy comes in the morning" (NASB). Suffering is not eternal. Importantly, God promises that there will be joy even in times of struggle. These moments become lifelines of grace allowing us to catch a glimpse of the time when all suffering will be gone.

But what of those not delivered as they would hope? It is naïve to think that every child being prayed for will be cured. It is naïve to assume that all of society will suddenly become understanding and accommodating for those with mental illness or autism. While not every suffering will be eliminated here on earth, the cessation of suffering, ultimately, will come at the end of this life. Hope is what bridges from the deepest struggles now to the eschaton toward which we look. Inherent in the resurrection is hope "that

2. Ibid., 241.

3. Markham, *Understanding Christian Doctrine*, 99.

death will not prevail, that nothingness does not have the last word. God promises to overcome it with life."[4] In this new life is hope.

But what of this hope? As Christians, we contend that hope is just as real as suffering. It is the very fiber of our beliefs. Hope is the doctrine that "stands knee deep in the history of this reality by yearning for the action of God to bring forth a new reality in which everything in this reality is reconciled and redeemed."[5] What Mary Elizabeth Moore expresses regarding youth is applicable here for those with disabilities. "Youth do yearn for much, but many have abandoned hope; impediments seem insurmountable."[6] Medical bills, social struggles, cognitive needs, and barriers to access can accumulate over time. While any one may be a struggle, the combination and unrelenting nature of societal response can make hope difficult to find. It however has not disappeared despite our inability to hold it through difficult seasons of life. God is the bearer of hope and believers have the privilege of getting to join God in that message to the world.

Eschatological hope, in particular, has a special place, inviting "us to place the struggles of human existence into an appropriate context. This life is not it. This does not mean we are promised 'pie in the sky,' but we are invited to place this moment of human existence into the context of eternity . . . . These realities invite us to participate in the promise of an ultimate reconciliation in the cosmos between the injustice suffered and the love promised."[7] Before we can even move our thoughts to eternity, we must get through today and each day that follows in this life. Hope has something to say for the now just as much as for the not yet.

Hope carries with it the possibility of all that God desires, a world that is at peace, fulfilled, whole—in short, perfect. Hope is rooted in the earliest of biblical texts. It is a strong part of our Christian heritage. Over the course of time, the church has brought hope with greater and lesser degrees of success. Still, the call for hope, for something better than what currently is has been present. One such clear call to the church comes from Walter Rauschenbusch in the early 1900s. While the context is a century ago, through the lens of disability, the concept still rings true. "Our chief interest in any millennium is the desire for a social order in which the worth and freedom of every least human being will be honored and protected;

4. Root, *Unlocking Mission*, 78.

5. Ibid., 64.

6. Moore, "Yearnings, Hopes, and Visions," 109.

7. Markham, *Understanding Christian Doctrine*, 99.

in which the brotherhood of man will be expressed in the common possession of the economic resources of society; and in which the spiritual good of humanity will be set high above the private profit interests of all materialistic groups. We hope for such an order for humanity as we hope for heaven ourselves."[8] The hope is for a better society where all are honored and protected as much as there is hope for the afterlife in heaven. We don't check out of the suffering of this world simply because this is temporary. Neither do we give into despair, ignoring the promise of the eschaton. It is a hope for the now and the not yet. It is into this hope that we are called. But just how does this dual manifestation of hope take place? It begins in creation, which was declared good by God. Shortly after creation, sin twisted what was intended and hope was hidden. God, being true to his nature, continued to pursue us and came in human form. Hope is then revealed in the glory of Christ. It is "in contrast to the creation of the world out of nothing, creation ex nihilo, resurrection is transformation or creation ex vetera ('creation out of something old'); yet the power of God's creation is at work in both instances."[9] Hope reminds us all that suffering is not the end of the story. God created and God redeems.

We live in the tension between suffering and hope every day. In my own family, we experience the tension as my mother ages and learns to live every day with multiple sclerosis. A couple of years ago, I took her to the hospital for what she believed was a knee problem, but seemed to me to be much more. In three days, she went from being able to walk, to excruciating pain and hallucinations. She was released from the first hospital prematurely. Left untreated for what truly ailed her, every major system in her body began to shut down, and we had to return to the hospital. I had two small children, was pregnant, underemployed, and struggling deeply. Days turned into weeks which turned into months, with us not knowing how this would end. We had relocated our lives, taken a major hit on our careers so that we could honor my parents and help as my mom's disability worsened. What I encountered, however, never quite felt like we were helping. It was more like living and doing what one has to do when family is in need. It was not a noble act. There were days I longed for an office and normal teaching career. There were days I wondered if I were doing any good at all being here. Overwhelmed, exhausted, and seemingly facing the death of my mother, I knew our family was suffering. I also knew this was not the end of the story.

8. Rauschenbusch, *A Theology for the Social Gospel*, 224.

9. Peters, "Where are We Going?," 353.

Were she to have died, I would have been heartbroken, but she would be out of pain. Were she to live I would still have her, but her life would once again be challenging, at a new level of normal that would include decreased mobility and possible cognitive damage. The latter is what took place. It was what I hoped for. I am, however, acutely aware that what I hoped for would bring new challenges and pain for my mom. What I ultimately hope for is a body that cooperates with her mind, free from pain and daily struggle. It is into this hope that I lean as I seek to live in the now and the not yet, the place of suffering, knowing one day it will end.

This experience with my mom living with an intensified disability taught me a lesson for which I could previously say the words but am only now coming to know. The nature of suffering for one can be the nature of hope for another. For Christians, these two concepts are intrinsically linked. They simultaneously seem worlds apart and like the closest of friends. We need only to look to the cross to see God suffering, and to know that hope for all eternity is being secured in that horrific act. The hope didn't make the crucifixion hurt any less. Hope does not eliminate the pain of suffering. That is an oft-held misconception. Hope, rather, reorients the suffering, bringing respite and strength.

The idea that all disabilities bring an endless parade of suffering for all is not rooted in reality. Those who live with disabilities—whether having a disability themselves or being close with those who do—will quickly tell you suffering is only a part of the story. Erna Albertz wrote an article in response to Richard Dawkins's statement about a mother's moral obligation to abort a child with Down syndrome. As mentioned previously, his argument is based on the belief that the person with Down syndrome would never experience happiness. They would only experience suffering and bring suffering to the family and society. Albertz very honestly wrote of the struggles with her own sister with Down syndrome. She wrote of the absolute gift that her sister is as she brings joy to her family and community. Albertz posed this poignant question, "How are we to determine who suffers more: a child with disabilities who possesses an uncomplicated joy in life, or an intellectually gifted child who has difficulty forging relationships?"[10] The answer of course is that we can't. Many people with disabilities have deep friendships, dreams, interests, family, and contributions to offer that make the world a better place. There are times when those with disabilities lives unencumbered by the noise of the world and

10. Albertz, "Pursuing Happiness," 18.

are able to hear God's still, small voice better than those of us who are typical who juggle responsibilities. It is a naïve assumption that all those with disabilities suffer to the point of misery. It is possible to suffer *and* live a satisfying and productive life.

Joni Eareckson Tada addresses this same concept of suffering from a different angle. She writes of the suffering brought not by individual pain or despair, but by discrimination and abuse in society. The temptation, if you do not know Joni's story, is to assume she is a woman who clearly has not experienced much based on her words. The assumption would be incorrect. She, perhaps more than most of us, is able to articulate first hand the reality of suffering society's input and influence. As a teenager, she became a quadriplegic after a diving accident. The road has not been easy, but she has lived and is still living with the consequences of a society that does not know what to do with her or others like her. She, however, also found hope in Christ in the midst of suffering and embraced that identity rather than the identity of a victim. In her own words:

> It is important to note that *suffering* does not necessarily have the same connotations as "being a *victim.*" Many people with disabilities do not consider themselves victims any more than the rest of humankind. While they acknowledge the real suffering that can result from disability, it is incorrect to generalize that all people with disabilities are victims. Unfortunately, more suffering comes *not* as the result of disability, but as a consequence of the attitudes and actions of individuals and society.[11]

Accepting this position, those in society who suffer, those with disabilities who suffer, are better able to identify with Christ. Christ suffered in life being misunderstood, rejected, questioned by family and friends, and ultimately dying on the cross. Jesus experienced the consequences of attitudes and actions of society that were harmful and led to his suffering. Jesus also knew of hope and extends this gift to us. "Hope finds in Christ not only a consolation in suffering, but also the protest of the divine promise against suffering. If Paul calls death the 'last enemy' (1 Cor 15:26), then the opposite is also true: that the risen Christ, and with him the resurrection hope, must be declared to be the enemy of death and of a world that puts up with death .... Those who hope in Christ can no longer put up with reality as it is, but begin to suffer under it, to contradict it."[12] Molt-

11. Tada and Bundy, *Beyond Suffering*, 92.
12. Moltmann, "Eschatological Theology," 164.

mann contends that this hope calls all individual believers and certainly the church to continually seek "new impulses towards the realization of righteousness, freedom, and humanity here in the light of the promised future that is to come."[13] The hope is always for something better today, tomorrow, and for the eternity to come.

Society does not always know what to do with someone with a disability. This is to be expected as there are many possible disabilities and ways in which they manifest. In this sense, just like with any individual, we need to get to know someone with a disability and accommodate their needs in a way that allows them to flourish. To learn what to do with someone with a disability requires for us to first see and hear them, to know they are human and treat them as such and to value all they have to contribute. The struggle that brings suffering enters in when society excludes, discriminates, and devalues those with disabilities. The rate of abuse for those with disabilities is higher than for the general population. In fact it is three times as high as the rate for those without any impairment.[14] Nazi Germany in World War II notoriously euthanized many with disabilities for being impure and not contributing to society. And yet, God is still God. His attributes have not changed. How then do we reconcile what we profess to be true with the reality we experience? Stanley Grenz offers this option, "Hope is possible, for God will bring his purposes to pass and is using even the evils of life in this process . . . (Psalm 73:16–28)."[15] The sovereignty of God is real, and it is in his nature to bring about what is just and right. Sometimes, perhaps most times, this takes longer than we as people would like. God is having to work with the world before him to bring hope of what is not yet, and to bring hope that one day, all will be as God intended. Until then, we cling to the audacious idea of hope knowing this world is not the end of the story.

It is difficult to know what exactly the hope of the eschaton will bring. What we have are clues more than descriptions or explanations. Along with paths of gold and pearly gates, we will have each other. Having one another includes those with disabilities as well as those who are typically abled. In sermons, the eschaton is most often presented as flawless: no pain, no suffering, no more tears, and all restored as it should be. The difficulty

13. Ibid., 164.

14. The difficulty at this point is that we now have evidence to show this to be true, and yet, the rate of abuse remains. The following three articles show this trend over time: Stalker and McArthur, "Child abuse"; Sullivan and Knutson, "Child maltreatment"; and Sullivan and Knutson, "Maltreatment and disabilities."

15. Grenz, *Theology for the Community of God*, 161.

is in knowing just what it means for "all to be as it should be" having never known nor experienced it ourselves. What we do know is what Scripture reveals. Revelation 21:4 says, "He will wipe every tear from their eyes. There will be no more death or mourning or crying or pain, for the old order of things has passed away." It does not say that all bodies will become typical bodies, all minds will become typical minds. It says that pain and mourning and death will be gone. Importantly, it also says that the old order will have passed away. Jesus revealed this over and over in two complementary teachings: the first will be last and the last will be first; and the foolish of this world will shame the wise. The kingdom is turned upside down and all we once knew is reversed.

This reversal is perhaps most clear in Luke 14. Luke wrote constantly of those who will be included in God's kingdom who were otherwise considered unworthy: women, the poor, sinners, Samaritans, and those with disabilities. The setting of this parable is a banquet in which Jesus has just made an impression on the powerful leaders in attendance by healing a man before the meal. As Jesus watched the leaders posture for places at the table, he shared the parable of the great banquet. Note that the parable includes those with disabilities. It is not a question of whether or not they will be included; they are included. The audience are those who are prestigious and powerful. Jesus knows this and masterfully tells the story in a way that they are able to follow to the end. He begins with their assumption that the noble and powerful will first be invited. All they had to do was look around the room and congratulate one another on making the cut! Jesus continues to unfold the parable revealing it was not they who will sit in places of honor at the banquet of the king, but those who were crippled, lame, and blind. The message is clear. The roles have been reversed. Amos Yong takes this one step further, noting that not only are those with disabilities present at the banquet, but they are present in their bodies as-is, disabilities and all.[16] Yong rightly notes "that the honoring of people with disabilities here doesn't follow our thanking God that they are no longer disabled—that would be easy enough for us to do. Instead the disabled are honored as people who have disabilities at the eschatological banquet—that is much more challenging for our normate assumptions."[17] Plainly, disabilities are not necessarily cured or hidden in the eschaton. Those with disabilities are, however, the recipients of places of honor. Just as the resurrected Jesus bears

16. Yong, *The Bible, Disability, and the Church*, 132–34.
17. Ibid., 134.

marks of the crucifixion living as the disabled God, those with disabilities are fully present, bearing the marks of their bodies with honor.

The interplay between suffering and hope is a complicated one. Suffering can be all-consuming, making daily tasks of life burdensome. Hope enters in and reorients the place of suffering, subordinating it to the promise of God's future. Those with disabilities need not dream of a day when they are other than they were created to be. What once was wise, is now foolish. The old order has been reversed and the new kingdom will be present free of suffering and full of honor.

Questions for Reflection and Ministerial Application

1. In what ways might the church enter into suffering with those with disabilities?

2. In what ways might the church be a bearer of hope for those with disabilities?

3. How were you challenged reading the complicated relationship between suffering and hope?

11 ⸺⸺⸺⸺⸺⸺⸺⸺⸺⸺⸺⸺

CONCLUSION
Who's in and who's out—A final word

> "When we live at the center, that's where we discover our neigh-
> bor, and ourselves, and where we discover that we are children
> of God."—Jaco Hamman

S ITTING DOWN TO WRITE this conclusion has been surprisingly difficult.
Even as I search for the words I get interrupted, repeatedly. The most
recent interruption was to go and repair the wheelchair my mom uses every
day. Here I am at the end of this work that has been stirring in my soul for
well over a decade and I was frustrated at yet another interruption when it
was a task that invited me to live the very theology I am advocating. I am
aware of the weight of what it is I am advocating here. I am also aware that
it is good and right, even when it is difficult. Once I realized that, I took a
deep breath and settled into the moment. Of all people, I want for my own
mother to feel included and important, as if she is worth every bit of extra
effort and that I have enough to give without worrying whether I will run
out. And yet, I do struggle. I do get tired. I do become overwhelmed with the
seemingly endless tasks that are added to lists of basic caregiving for those
in my life with disabilities. It is for them that this conclusion must be written. I write this conclusion not to offer a last-ditch effort to convince anyone
of the validity of what I have been saying. Rather, I write it as a reminder
of the gift that I have been given to put these thoughts down in writing. I
write it as a reminder that these thoughts must move beyond mere thought
and create the very fabric of my daily activities. By the world's standards,
my life is far from perfect. Yet, with perfection redefined, it is full, whole,
vibrant, and unpredictable. Perfection is no longer defined as flawlessness.
It is defined by the measure of all that God provides in seemingly hopeless

circumstances. It is the hope-filled invitation to constantly be turning and moving toward Jesus in all we say, do, think, and feel.

Throughout this book the goal has been to consider theology in a way that moves beyond mere welcome towards genuine inclusion. Much to my surprise, as I worked on each area over the past decade, I thought I was working on theology and disability. What I learned was that my theology was simply becoming more biblical and inclusive of all people. It moved from a checklist of what it meant to be a good Christian, church, or theologian, to a reorientation and awareness that we are all a work in process. Some of my friends can't tell you in any sophisticated terms about the Trinity or what God did on the cross, but they can model kindness and pray for others in need. Some of my friends use very colorful language that would not be accepted in most church circles, while giving sacrificially of their time and talents for others to hear the gospel. Some of my friends have been told they could not be baptized or be in church leadership as they did not have the ability to explain what any particular theological point meant in detail, yet they know not to gossip or tell jokes at the expense of others.

Ultimately, God alone knows who is "in" and who is "out." Still, this conversation continues and both Scripture and theology are consistently disrupting what we once thought. It is through God's revelation that we can declare the inclusion and impact of those with disabilities on what we believe and how we are to live this out.

Paul Hiebert, a mathematically trained missiologist, addressed the idea of inclusion in his influential work discussing bounded sets and centered sets.[1] Bounded sets are those that have uniform, static, clear standards that comprise distinct boundaries. In other words, it is easy to tell who is "in" and who is "out" based on a distinct set of criteria that determine the boundary. Those who are "in" are found inside the boundary because they can check off each criterion on the checklist. Those who are outside the boundary are not included in the set. They cannot check off every criterion of what it means to be "in." So, what does that look like in terms of defining what it means to be Christian? For many of us it has meant asking about the criteria that are important to our church or denomination. Imagine the scenario in which an elder at the church mentally evaluates a member of the church. Has he said the sinner's prayer? Check. Has he given his heart to Jesus? Check. Does he believe all the "right" things (depending on the denomination's doctrine)? Check. Does he live a life consistent with one

1. Hiebert, "Conversion, Culture, and Cognitive Categories."

who has been Spirit-filled? No check. Hmm. We have some questions about whether this person is *really* a Christian. Or imagine the conversation was about perfection. Are you flawless? Are you sin-free? Are you without blemish? Wow. That's a high hurdle to clear.

Centered sets, on the other hand, are those whose defining characteristic is a "center or reference point and the relationship of things to that center; members are things that move toward, or are in relationship to, a common center or reference point."[2] So, imagine a bull's-eye, where the center is the prototypical member of the category, and everything else is in a dynamic relationship with that center point either moving towards or away from it. Imagine that scenario again with the church elder. The questions now are simplified, so to speak, to one central question: are you moving towards or away from Jesus? The focus is less on being able to articulate doctrine and reinforces the idea of one's relationship with Jesus. So if our friends with disabilities cannot explain what happens in the atonement but they love Jesus, who are we to exclude them from our understanding of Christian?

Hiebert used this mathematical notion to look at what missionaries had been discussing for generations: what does it mean to be a Christian? We may never know whether Hiebert knew that in articulating a model of inclusion for newly converted Christians in non-Western cultures that he was paving the way for including those disabilities.

Let's end this by circling back to the premise of this book. Let's redefine perfect. The old definition of perfect may be about flawlessness, and it may be a very high hurdle to clear, but it is something I am comfortable considering. Perfect is, in my old definition, something a lot like me. Certainly it is not exactly me. I know I cannot live up to that standard. But it is a lot *like* me. Perfect is the best version of everything that makes me comfortable. In the new definition of perfect, however, I realize the depth and breadth of God's vision of perfect. It's not about requiring others to look like me, sound like me, think like me. It is about making room at the table and doing the slow and beautiful work of getting to see glimpses of God in those he created. For friends with disabilities, this means not only knowing in the depths of their being that they are valued but that the community that surrounds them knows this, too, and acts accordingly. *That* is perfect.

2. Yoder et al., "Understanding Christian Identity."

BIBLIOGRAPHY

Albertz, Erna. "Pursuing Happiness: How my sister with Down syndrome can help Richard Dawkins boost the sum of human joy." *Plough Quarterly* 10 (Autumn 2016) 16–24.

Amundsen, Darrell. *Medicine, Science, and Faith in the Ancient and Medieval Worlds.* Baltimore: Johns Hopkins University Press, 1996.

Atkinson, James. "Vocation." In *New Dictionary of Theology*, edited by David F. Wright, et al., eds., 711. Downers Grove, IL: InterVarsity, 1998.

Barth, Karl. *Church Dogmatics.* 4 vols. Edinburgh: T & T Clark, 1958.

Battles, Michael. "How Should We Live?" In *Essentials of Christian Theology*, edited by William Placher, 280–96. Louisville: Westminster John Knox, 2003.

Beck, Richard. *Unclean: Meditations on Purity, Hospitality, and Mortality.* Eugene, OR: Cascade, 2011.

Bonhoeffer, Dietrich. *Life Together.* San Francisco: Harper SanFrancisco, 1954.

Bos, Johanna W. H. "The Way of Hesed." In *And Show Steadfast Love: A Theological Look at Grace, Hospitality, Disabilities, and the Church*, edited by Lewis Merrick, 9–16. Louisville: Presbyterian, 1993.

Brunner, Emil. *Revelation and Reason.* Translated by Olive Wyon. Philadelphia: Westminster, 1946.

Burd, Deborah, and Dennis Barta. "No Limits: Answering God's Call to Ministry When You Have a Disability." *The Journal on the Christian Institute on Disability* 4.2 (Fall/Winter 2015) 75–97.

Caspary, Almut. "The Patristic Era: Early Christian attitudes toward the Disfigured Outcast." In *Disability in the Christian Tradition: A Reader*, edited by Brian Brock and John Swinton, 24–64. Grand Rapids: Eerdmans, 2012.

Creamer, Deborah. *Disability and Christian Theology: Embodied Limits and Constructive Possibilities.* New York: Oxford University Press, 2009.

Dawkins, Richard. "Abortion & Down Syndrome: An Apology for the Letting Slip the Dogs of Twitterwar." https://richarddawkins.net/2014/08/abortion-down-syndrome-an-apology-for-letting-slip-the-dogs-of-twitterwar/.

Eiesland, Nancy. *The Disabled God: Toward a Liberatory Theology of God.* Nashville: Abingdon, 1994.

Elwell, Walter, ed. *Evangelical Dictionary of Theology.* 2nd ed. Grand Rapids: Baker, 2001.

Erickson, Millard. *Christian Theology.* Grand Rapids: Baker, 1991.

Erskine, Noel Leo. "How Do We Know What To Believe?" In *Essentials of Christian Theology,* edited by William Placher, 280–96. Louisville: Westminster John Knox, 2003.

Fernandez, Eleazar. *Reimagining the Human: Theological Anthropology in Response to Systemic Evil.* St. Louis: Chalice, 2004.

Grenz, Stanley. "How Do We Know What to Believe?" In *Essentials of Christian Theology,* edited by William Placher, 280–96. Louisville: Westminster John Knox, 2003.

———. *The Social God and the Relational Self: A Trinitarian Theology of the Imago Dei.* Louisville: Westminster John Knox, 2001.

———. *Theology for the Community of God.* Nashville: Broadman Holman, 1994.

Gunton, Colin. *The One, the Three and the Many.* Cambridge: Cambridge University Press, 1993.

Hamman, Jaco. *A Play-Full Life: Slowing Down and Seeking Peace.* Cleveland: Pilgrim, 2011.

Hauerwas, Stanley, and Jean Vanier. *Living Gently in a Violent World: the Prophetic Witness of Weakness.* Downers Grove, IL: InterVarsity, 2008.

Heuser, Stefan. "The Human Condition as Seen from the Cross: Luther and Disability." In *Disability in the Christian Tradition,* edited by Brian Brock and John Swinton, 184–215. Grand Rapids: Eerdmans, 2012.

Hiebert, Paul. "Conversion, Culture, and Cognitive Categories." *Gospel in Context* (October 1978) 24–29.

Jacober, Amy. "Church and the Unmaking of Violence in the Experiences of Those with Disabilities." Presented at the Religious Education Association, 2015, Chicago.

———. "Ostensibly Welcome: Exploratory Research on the Youth Ministry Experiences of Families of Teenagers with Disabilities." *The Journal of Youth Ministry* 6.1 (Fall 2007) 167–81.

Jacober, Amy, and Mindi Godfrey. "Hospitality and a God-given Identity." Presented at International Association for the Study of Youth Ministry Conference 2015, London. Unpublished.

Jewett, Paul. *Man as Male and Female.* Grand Rapids: Eerdmans, 1975.

Knight, Douglas, and Amy Jill Levine. *The Meaning of the Bible: What the Jewish Scriptures and Christian Old Testament Can Teach Us.* New York: Harper One, 1989.

Kraybill, Donald. *The Upside Down Kingdom.* Scottdale, PA: Herald, 1978.

Lehrer, Jonah. "Accept Defeat: the Neuroscience of screwing up." *Wired Magazine* (January 2010). http://www.wired.com/magazine/2009/12/fail_accept_defeat/.

Loder, James. *The Logic of the Spirit.* San Francisco: Jossey-Bass, 1998.

MacIntyre, Alasdair. *After Virtue: A Study in Moral Theory.* 2nd ed. Notre Dame, IN: University of Notre Dame Press, 1984.

———. *Dependent Rational Animals: Why Human Beings Need the Virtues.* Chicago: Open Court, 1998.

Markham, Ian S. *Understanding Christian Doctrine.* Oxford: Blackwell, 2008.

Maston, T. B. *Both-And: A Maston Reader, Selected Readings from the Writings of T. B. Maston.* Edited by W. Tillman, R. Taylor, and L. Brewer. Fort Worth, TX: T. B. Maston Foundation, 2011.

McClendon, James Wm. *Doctrine: Systematic Theology,* vol. 2. Nashville: Abingdon, 1994.

McNair, Jeff. "The Power of Those Who Seem Weaker: People with Disabilities In the Church." *The Journal of the Christian Institute on Disability* 3.1 (Spring/Summer 2014) 93–107.

———. "What Would Be Better?" *The Journal of the Institute on Disability* 1.1 (Fall/ Winter 2012) 12–22.

Migliore, Daniel. *Faith Seeking Understanding: An Introduction to Christian Theology.* 2nd ed. Grand Rapids: Eerdmans, 2004.

Moltmann, Jürgen. "Eschatological Theology." In *A Map of Twentieth Century Theology,* edited by Carl Braaten and Robert Jenson, 147–78. Minneapolis: Fortress, 1995.

Moore, Mary Elizabeth. "Yearnings, Hopes, and Visions" In *Children, Youth, and Spirituality in a Troubling World,* edited by Mary Elizabeth Moore and Almeda Wright, 108–22. St. Louis: Chalice, 2008.

Peters, Ted. "Where are We Going?" In *Essentials of Christian Theology,* edited by William Placher, 280–96. Louisville: Westminster John Knox, 2003

Rauschenbusch, Walter. *Dare We Be Christians? A Classic Treatise on Love.* Cleveland: Pilgrim, 1993.

———. *A Theology for the Social Gospel.* New York: Macmillan Company, 1918.

Reynolds, Thomas E. *Vulnerable Communion: A Theology of Disability and Hospitality.* Grand Rapids: Brazos, 2008.

Root, Andrew. *Unlocking Mission and Eschatology in Youth Ministry.* Grand Rapids: Zondervan, 2012.

Schipper, Jeremy. *Disability Studies and the Hebrew Bible: Figuring Mephibosheth In The David Story.* New York: T & T Clark, 2006.

Smith, Mark. *The Origins of Biblical Monotheism: Israel's Polytheistic Background and the Ugaritic Texts.* Oxford: Oxford University Press, 2001.

Stalker, K., and K. McArthur. "Child abuse, child protection and disabled children: a review of recent research." *Child Abuse Review* 21 (2012) 24–40.

Stevens, R. Paul. "Vocational Guidance." In *The Complete Book of Everyday Christianity,* edited by Robert Banks and R. Paul Stevens. Downers Grove, IL: InterVarsity, 1997.

Sullivan, P. M., and J. Knutson. "The association between child maltreatment and disabilities in a hospital-based epidemiological study." *Child Abuse and Neglect* 22.4 (1998) 271–88.

———. "Maltreatment and disabilities: a population based epidemiological study." *Child Abuse and Neglect* 24.10 (2000) 1257–73.

Swinton, John. "Disability, Ableism, and Disablism." In *The Wiley-Blackwell Companion to Practical Theology,* edited by B. Miller-McLemore, 443–51. New York: Oxford University Press, 2011.

Tada, Joni Eareckson, and Steve Bundy. *Beyond Suffering: A Christian View on Disability Ministry.* Agoura Hills, CA: The Christian Institute on Disability, 2011.

Taylor, Barbara Brown. *Speaking of Sin: The Lost Language of Salvation.* New York: Cowley, 2000.

Tickle, Phyllis. *The Age of the Spirit: How the Ghost of an Ancient Controversy is Shaping the Church.* Grand Rapids: Baker, 2014.

Tillich, Paul. *Systematic Theology,* vol. 2. Chicago: The University of Chicago Press, 1957.

Tumeinski, Marc, and Jeff McNair. "What Would Be Better?: Social Role Valorization and the Development of Ministry to Persons Affected by Disability." *The Journal of the Christian Institute on Disability* 1.1 (Fall/Winter 2012) 11–22.

Walker, Robert, ed. *Speaking Out: Gifts of Ministering Undeterred by Disabilities.* Charleston, SC: Create Space, 2012.

Wannenwetsch, Bernd. "'My Strength is Made Perfect in Weakness': Bonhoeffer and the War over Disabled Life." In *Disability in the Christian Tradition: A Reader,* edited by Brian Brock and John Swinton, 353–90. Grand Rapids: Eerdmans, 2012.

White, George. "People with Disabilities in Christian Community." *The Journal of the Christian Institute on Disability* 3.1 (Spring/Summer 2014) 12–35.

Wright, Almeda. "The Power of Testimonies." In *Children, Youth, and Spirituality in a Troubling World,* edited by Mary Elizabeth Moore and Almeda Wright, 182–95. St. Louis: Chalice, 2008.

Yoder, Michael, Michael Lee, Jonathan Ro, and Robert Priest. "Understanding Christian Identity in Terms of Bounded and Centered Set Theory in the Writings of Paul G. Hiebert." *Trinity Journal* 30.2 (Fall 2009) 177–88.

Yong, Amos. *The Bible, Disability, and the Church: A New Vision of the People of God.* Grand Rapids: Eerdmans, 2011.

———. *Theology and Down Syndrome: Reimagining Disability in Late Modernity.* Waco, TX: Baylor University Press, 2007.

Zirshcky, Andrew. *Beyond the Screen: Youth Ministry for the Connected But Alone Generation.* Nashville: Abingdon, 2015.

AUTHOR INDEX

SUBJECT INDEX

humanity, 10, 13, 18n4, 19, 22, 24, 36–37,
46, 52, 95, 98

IDD, 10, 23, 33, 34, 40, 41, 50, 69, 85, 88,
95, 99
illness, 39, 82, 84, 85–87, 93
imago dei, 37, 39
injury, 12, 83–84
injustice, 4–5, 47, 65, 94

Jesus, 7, 18, 21–23, 30, 38, 44, 47–49, 52,
56, 64, 67–76, 80–84, 89–90, 97,
99, 102–3
justice, 19, 73

kingdom, 1, 6, 22, 73, 88, 99–100

L'Arche, 13, 35–36, 52
leadership, 4, 6–7, 67, 78, 90–91, 102
love, 2, 7, 16–17, 19, 21–22, 28, 30–31,
32, 34, 42–44, 46–47, 50–51, 56,
63–65, 66, 69–72, 74, 76, 92, 94,
103

member, 6, 13, 18–19, 21–22, 24, 37,
50–54, 57–58, 62, 67, 102–3
mental illness, 82, 86–87, 93
minister, 1, 5, 6, 7, 75
mistake, 6, 14, 19, 27– 31, 35, 42, 60, 67
monotheism, 18, 36

normal, 34, 53, 62, 95–96
normalcy, 11–12

perfect, 1–4, 21, 23, 25, 34, 36, 51, 67–69,
73, 94, 101, 103
privilege, 11, 30, 45, 62, 94

reconciliation, 24, 29, 62, 94
redefine, 67, 101, 103
revelation, 7–11, 13–14, 19, 29, 37, 68–
69, 79–81, 93, 102
rhythm, 54–56, 69, 75
righteous, 29, 93
righteousness, 19, 63, 98
ritual, 7, 54–56, 69, 75

scripture, 2–3, 9, 18, 20, 24, 36, 46, 56–
57, 63, 67–69, 78–91, 99, 102
Shema, 17
sin, 6, 22, 24, 28–30, 41–47, 56, 58, 64,
65, 72, 82–83, 87, 89, 93, 95, 99,
102–3
Social Role Valorization, 53–54
sovereignty, 26–31, 45, 98
stigma, 46, 87
suffering, 24, 25n2, 31, 45–46, 73, 84, 88,
92–100

Trinity, 17–24, 28, 30, 37, 39, 102

unclean, 21, 22, 86

vocation, 68, 74–77

worship, 18, 24, 55–57, 66–71, 73, 75, 81

SCRIPTURE INDEX

CPSIA information can be obtained
at www.ICGtesting.com
Printed in the USA
LVHW091312010520
654862LV00007B/1874